HISTORICAL CATASTROPHES: EARTHQUAKES

Addison-Wesley

EARTH

by Billye Walker Brown and Walter R. Brown

HISTORICAL CATASTROPHES:

QUAKES

Titles in the Historical Catastrophe Series

Text Copyright © 1974 by Billye Walker Brown and Walter R. Brown
Illustrations Copyright © 1974 by Addison-Wesley Publishing Company, Inc.
All Rights Reserved
Addison-Wesley Publishing Company, Inc.
Reading, Massachusetts 01867
Printed in the United States of America

ISBN 0-201-00546-8
EFGHIJ-WZ-79

Library of Congress Cataloging in Publication Data

Brown, Billye Walker.
  Historical catastrophes: earthquakes.

  SUMMARY: Discusses major earthquakes throughout
history and the means developed to measure their force.
  "An Addisonian Press book."
  1. Earthquakes—Juvenile literature. [1. Earth-
quakes] I. Brown, Walter R., 1929–   joint author.
II. Title.
QE539.B76   551.2'2   73-15617
ISBN 0–201–00546–8

CONTENTS

ACKNOWLEDGEMENTS

Photographs in this book are reproduced courtesy of the following institutions:

pages 2–3, 44, 45, 53, 55: Environmental Science Services Administration

page 17: source unknown

pages 34–35: early engraving, source unknown

page 50: M.L. Fuller, U.S. Geological Survey

pages 60–61: The Bettmann Archive

pages 64, 65: G.K. Gilbert, U.S. Geological Survey

page 71: J.R. Balsley, U.S. Geological Survey

page 77: U.S. Geological Survey

page 87: source unknown

pages 132–133, 162, 163, 169, 172, 173: National Oceanic and Atmospheric Administration

page 141: United Press International

pages 157, 173: Coast and Geodetic Survey

FOREWORD

ALMOST EVERY DAY, it seems, the newspapers report an earthquake somewhere in the world. Most of these are only tremors that are ignored by those people who feel them, if they are felt at all. Some are more severe and may cause people to feel anxious for a few moments. It depends somewhat upon where the earthquake is felt. Residents of Southern California, for instance, are so used to mild and moderate tremors that they hardly pay attention to them. People who live in Chile on the other hand may feel panic as a mild tremor reminds them of recent devastation of their cities and countryside by a major quake. But several times each year earthquakes smash through the earth with enough force to destroy buildings, cut people off from the rest of the world, and sometimes kill hundreds of human beings.

Who can help but be fascinated by this tremendous, unpredictable force, which can be greater than hundreds of atomic bombs? Who can help but wonder what causes these catastrophes and why they appear in some parts of the world and leave other parts untouched?

The natural interest that we have in earthquakes has been held by people throughout the ages. It is an interest that we share with the Greek philosopher Democritus, who lived 25 centuries ago, and with John Wesley, the 18th Century founder of the Methodist church. It is an interest that we share today with scientists and engineers who are studying the earth.

This book is the story of the search for answers to questions about earthquakes—their nature and cause, and how to predict and protect ourselves from them. It is the story of the earth itself—how it was formed and how it is changing. It is the story of the history of mankind—from the legend of Atlantis to tomorrow's newspaper headlines. These stories take place almost everywhere there are people living today—from Lisbon to San Francisco, and from Tokyo to Anchorage.

This book is also the story of the people whose lives have been disrupted suddenly, without warning, by an earthquake. You will read about a Portuguese king who cannot decide what to do after an earthquake destroys his capital city, causing him to lose control of his kingdom. A famous opera singer, afraid that the shocks of an earthquake might have damaged his voice, stands at the window of his hotel room and sings to the collapsing buildings of a ruined San Francisco. People who have survived the destruction of their homes rush to the docks in the hope that they will be rescued, only to drown when a huge sea wave smashes over them. The walls of an Italian prison fall, freeing thirty convicted murderers who try to rob a bank. Campers, asleep in a Montana campground, suddenly find themselves drowning in a flood released when an earthquake destroys a dam above them. French Marines dig for 40 hours in the rubble of a town in Morocco to save an American woman who has been buried alive. An earthquake in Chile launches a sea wave that kills 61 people in Hawaii and later kills 190 more in Japan.

But perhaps most importantly, this book is also the story of the future. Man's curiosity about the unknown has caused him to spend a great deal of time studying this force within our earth. Over the years, scientists have learned a lot about the causes of earthquakes. Building on this knowledge and using new techniques of research, we will eventually discover ways to protect ourselves from these catastrophes. Perhaps someday we will be able to build our cities so that they will be "earthquake proof." Perhaps we will discover how to predict exactly when and where an earthquake will strike. Or, as some people have suggested, we may even learn how to prevent earthquakes entirely.

Billye Walker Brown
Walter R. Brown

CHAPTER ONE

THE
UNSTABLE
EARTH

SEVEN-YEAR-OLD SONNY ULRICH and his father had anchored their boat deep inside beautiful Lituya Bay. They were 120 miles west of Juneau, Alaska, where the towering peaks of Mount Fairweather mark the border between Alaska and the Canadian province of British Columbia. The highest peak of Mount Fairweather, on the Alaskan side, stood more than 15,000 feet above them.

Lituya Bay is only about seven miles long. Its mouth is nearly closed by a long, narrow spit of land that is littered with rocks and covered by a low stand of evergreen trees and shrubs. Along the sides of the bay are the steep sides of low mountain ridges that are covered by evergreens. At the back of the bay, near the foot of Mount Fairweather, a wide, frozen river hangs over the water. Ice from this glacier falls into the bay during the summer months, dotting the water with small icebergs. Among the icebergs is a small island that pokes its head from the very center of the bay.

Many people visit the bay during the warmer months of the year. Some come to enjoy the natural beauty of the area and others come to fish in the bay's cold water. On the night of July 9, 1958, three fishing boats were anchored in the bay.

One of these boats was the 39-foot-long *Edrie*, which belonged to Sonny's father. Closer to the spit of land were two other boats, each with two people on board and each anchored. The sun was just going down and both of the Ulrichs were in their bunks, ready for sleep. The sounds of the night drifted softly across the bay to them.

Suddenly the calm night was broken by a loud hammering sound against the hull of the *Edrie*. Sonny and his father rushed out into the dim light and looked around them. The boat was tossing wildly and the waves smashed into its hull with increasingly louder sounds. An even louder roar came to them from the direction of Mount Fairweather.

They looked up at the huge mountain and thought they saw its peaks shiver. Clouds of snow and dust rose from dozens of places along its sides. Then they saw the glacier rise straight up into the air, hang there for a moment, and cascade down into the bay.

Forced ahead of the avalanche of snow, ice, and rock were tons of water that formed a wave more than 100 feet high. Sonny and his father watched in horror as the wave rushed across the bay and climbed high up the opposite wall. Then it fell back into the bay, reformed, and smashed across to the other shore. Each time, the wall of water came closer and closer to them.

Sonny's father quickly started the boat's motor and tried to pull in the anchor.

"It's too slow!" he yelled to Sonny over the roaring that came to them from all directions. "Get into a life jacket and hang on for dear life!"

Grabbing the microphone of the boat's radio, he broadcast a general call for help.

"MAYDAY! MAYDAY!" he shouted. "This is *Edrie* in Lituya Bay. All hell broke loose here. I think we've had it. Goodbye!"

Mr. Ulrich tried to pull the anchor loose by running the boat out to the end of the chain, but realized soon that it was no use. The wave was almost upon them. As the water drowned the island in the middle of the bay, he packed Sonny into a corner with several pillows, again told him to hang on tightly, and turned the boat directly into the wave.

As the face of the wave reached the *Edrie*, Mr. Ulrich drove the boat straight ahead into the ris-

ing water as far as the anchor chain would let him.
The boat rose with the wave until the chain finally
broke. Helplessly the boat swirled along with the
wave toward the other two boats still anchored
near the mouth of the bay. But the crest of the
wave had passed, and the *Edrie* settled back safely
into the tumbling waters of the bay.

Dodging floating trees and huge chunks of ice,
Sonny's father guided his boat out of the bay and
into the safety of the open ocean. There they
found the wreckage of the other boats that had
been their neighbors' that night. Both of the
people on one of the boats had been killed when
their boat smashed against the rocks of the spit.
Later the two people who had been on the second
boat were found alive. They had managed to
escape only seconds before their boat broke into
pieces against the rocks.

Sonny Ulrich, his father, and these two other
lucky people had managed to live through a major
earthquake.

People like to think of the earth as being very
solid and stable. But during one year perhaps one
million earthquakes will shake the earth's surface.
Most of these will be very minor shivers of the
crust and will be noticed only by scientists who
watch the sensitive *seismograph* instruments. These
instruments can feel and measure even the
slightest shock.

Some 300,000 of the earthquakes that occur in
any year will be strong enough to be felt by human
beings. Many of these, perhaps half, will not be

felt because they will occur under the ocean, so far from the shore that they will not disturb land-dwelling humans. Only a dozen or two earthquakes will be strong enough to damage buildings, destroy roads, disrupt communications, and cause the deaths of many hundreds of people.

It would seem logical that people have always wondered about the cause of earthquakes. Like modern people, earliest man must have thought of the earth as being solid and steady. But when he felt it shake and saw it suddenly crack open under his feet, he must have been frightened and tried to explain this strange, unusual behavior.

Before man developed scientific methods and instruments to explain earthquakes, people invented detailed and imaginative stories about why the earth should suddenly become unstable. Many of these tales are interwoven with the stories these people invented to explain why the earth itself did not fall. There were groups of people who thought (and some still believe) that the earth is held on the back of some huge animal and that earthquakes occur when this animal shifts its body. To many Moslems, it was a bull that supported the earth. Some Hindus suggested an elephant, while others thought that it might be a giant mole, like the smaller ones that burrow in the earth. The Algonquin Indians of North America pictured the earth on the back of a huge tortoise that occasionally shifted its weight as it slowly walked along. Because of the importance of the buffalo to them, the Dyaks of Borneo assumed that it was this ani-

mal that carried the earth; while the lamas of
Mongolia once suggested that the world rested on
the back of a giant frog.

Some of these stories become strangely com-
plicated. Some East African tribes, for example,
tell of a fish that swims in an ocean. On the back
of the fish is a large rock. And on the rock stands
a huge cow. The earth rests on one horn of this
cow and sometimes the cow becomes tired and
shifts the weight of the world to the other horn.
The result is an earthquake.

Snakes, being animals that are both mysterious
and live in the ground, are often blamed for
earthquakes. One group in India believed that the
earth was supported on the head of a large snake.
Naturally, the snake could not hold up such
weight for very long, so the earth would be passed
on to another snake and an earthquake would
result. For some unexplained reason, a total of
seven snakes were involved in this story.

Sometimes earthquakes are explained by stories
about animals that do not hold up the earth but
that live on the earth. On the island of Celebes,
in Indonesia, stories were told of a giant hog that
occasionally stopped to rub its back against an
even larger tree. In Japan a twitching whale, a
walking spider, and a flopping catfish have all
been blamed for causing earthquakes.

People of other cultures have blamed their gods
for earthquakes. The early Russian people who
lived near the Arctic Circle on Kamchatka Peninsula had a god named Tuil who rode across the

*A Greek myth explained
that earthquakes occurred when
Atlas shifted the world
on his shoulders.*

ice and snow by dog sled. Unfortunately, Tuil's dogs had fleas and often they would be forced to stop and scratch at the pests. When they did so, the earth would shake.

Legends of the ancient Greeks often were attempts to explain the earthquakes that are common around the Mediterranean Sea. Some stories blamed Atlas, who rebelled against the gods and was punished by having to bear the world on his shoulders. Other stories told of Atlas' brother, Prometheus, shaking the earth as he tried to free himself from the chains that bound him to Mount Caucasus. Or, since so many earthquakes seemed to occur near the sea, some stories blamed the sea god, Poseidon. Later, the Romans suggested that their god of the sea, Neptune, was the villain.

Many people around the earth today still believe that specific gods control the sea and are responsible for earthquakes and the so-called "tidal waves" that often follow them. In South America as recently as 1960, a primitive tribe of people called Araucanians tried to stop the shaking of the earth and calm the waves of the Pacific Ocean by offering a human sacrifice to their god of the sea. A six-year-old boy was killed and his blood poured onto the incoming tide.

By the Fifth Century, B.C., many of the Greek philosophers were trying to explain the mysteries of nature without blaming supernatural beings. For some reason, these early scientists came to believe that there was some relationship between earthquakes and rainfall. One philosopher, Anaxagoras, believed a mysterious gas was carried into the earth by the rain. Earthquakes, he said, were caused when this gas tried to return to its natural place, the air. Another Greek named Democritus, who lived at about the same time as Anaxagoras, disagreed. He believed that earthquakes were caused by the rainwater itself, or perhaps by water seeping into the ground from the ocean or from large lakes. A century later, Aristotle declared that the shaking of the earth was caused by pockets of air struggling to escape from underground caves.

A few early writers spoke of the earth as if it were alive. About the time that Jesus lived, the Roman poet Ovid explained that the earth trembled because it was afraid of being burned by the sun which had wandered too near. Shakespeare said, in his famous play *Macbeth*, "Some say the earth was feverish and did shake."

The Book of Matthew describes a tremendous earthquake that occurred on the day Jesus was crucified. From that time until the 18th Century, nearly all Christians believed that earthquakes were a sign that God was displeased with someone or some group of people.

In Italy, shortly after the crucifixion, it was believed by some Christians that earthquakes were caused by Malco, the man who struck Jesus as he climbed Calvary. As punishment, God forced Malco to turn the post that supported the earth. Hoping that he could cause the earth to fall, Malco would strike the post, causing the entire earth to shake.

In the Sixth Century, Justinian I became emperor of the Byzantine Empire. Centered in Constantinople (now the Turkish city of Istanbul), the empire grew until Justinian I controlled almost all of the land around the Mediterranean Sea. Justinian was a harsh ruler and the death penalty was given for many crimes. Two crimes that called for the death penalty were irreverence toward God and "swearing by the hair of one's head." The reason given by the emperor for declaring these to be major crimes was that these practices were believed to provoke God to cause earthquakes.

A thousand years later, God was still being blamed for earthquakes. During the 17th Century in Europe, church leaders explained to their followers that earthquakes were signs that God was unhappy with the lack of morals of His people. In Rumania, some people believed that the earth rested on three pillars. These three pillars represented the three moral values of Faith, Hope, and Charity. When people failed to uphold any one of these three values, it was said, the earth lost part of its support and trembled.

Even some of the early scientists tended to see earthquakes as God's punishment for the sins of humans. Jan van Helmont, a famous chemist of the 17th Century, wrote, "An avenging angel strikes the air and the vibrations from the musical tone cause the earth to shake." And a British Royal Society publication of 1752 says that earthquakes occur only in places where people need punishment.

This idea is not completely dead. In 1930, the archbishop of Naples announced that a recent Italian quake was a sign that God was displeased by the immodesty of women and the general immorality of the people of Naples. And more recently, in 1946, the countries of Haiti and the Dominican Republic were struck by a particularly bad earthquake. Rather than being concerned with rescuing the people injured by the catastrophe, many of the survivors spent their time trying to appease God by walking around with ashes and rocks on their heads.

Modern *geologists*, scientists who study the earth, are the first to admit that they do not understand all there is to know about the cause of earthquakes. At one time, not very many years ago, it was believed by some geologists that earthquakes could be caused by the collapse of underground caverns, by meteorites smashing into the surface of the earth, or by the eruption of volcanoes. Any of these disturbances of the crust of the earth would, of course, cause the ground nearby to shake. But this would be felt only over a small area and would do little, if any, damage.

It is now a well accepted idea that all major earthquakes—those that are felt over a large area—are the result of rocks slipping along a crack, called a *fault*. This fault may be on the surface of the earth or it may be as deep as 400 miles beneath the surface.

What is not yet fully understood is *why* the rocks break and slip. Apparently the rocks under the surface are under tremendous pressures that, in some parts of the world, are slowly increasing. Earthquakes occur when these pressures become so great that the rocks finally crack and move. The question that geologists are now busily trying to answer is, "Where does the pressure come from?"

CHAPTER TWO

LISBON
NOVEMBER 1, 1755

LISBON WAS AN EXCITING PLACE to be during the autumn of 1755, especially if you were a young English boy on his first sea voyage. Robert Clarke had just celebrated his 14th birthday and in honor of this event Robert's father had offered to take the boy with him to Portugal. Captain Clarke was in command of the merchant ship *Northampton*. He was taking the ship on the short run from England to Lisbon with a special group of government representatives.

The ship sailed smoothly through the English Channel and across the Bay of Biscay. Young

Robert spent many happy hours watching his father chart their course or just roaming through the passageways of the vessel. The winds were favorable and, with all of her sails set, the *Northampton* rounded Cape Roxant in record time. To its left stood tree-shrouded cliffs above a pounding surf and to its right lay a sandbar that was almost awash in the rising tide. Seven miles up the bay, hidden from sight by the curving shore, towered the ancient city of Lisbon.

Carefully, Captain Clarke eased his huge ship into the narrows between the shoreline and the sandbar. The tide, trapped between the two points of land, carried them smoothly and safely into the Bay of Oeiras.

"The bay is actually the mouth of the Tagus River," Robert's father explained as they drifted slowly along under shortened sail. "The sandbars back there form a natural breakwater, so that the entire bay is one large, safe harbor."

Although some distance away, the wooded shores could now be seen on both sides of the ship. Robert stood at the railing and watched the ships that crowded the large harbor. A few were gunboats from a dozen navies, there to protect the interests of the foreigners who lived in Portugal. Many merchant ships were anchored in sheltered parts of the bay or had moved along toward the still-hidden city as did the *Northampton*. Captain Clarke told Robert that these large ships were returning from the gold fields of Brazil, or from the colonies on the islands of the Caribbean or in America. Making their way toward the markets on shore, small barges full of fruits and vegetables and fishing boats, called smacks, darted in and out among the larger ships.

"There is Belem Tower," Captain Clarke said, pointing to a large building standing on a point of land that had appeared on their port side. "It is a palace where the king takes his family when they grow tired of living in the city. And next to it—the smaller building—is Jeronimos Convent. When we round that point of land, we will be in Lisbon."

The captain turned his attention to the business of picking up a pilot from a small boat that had come to meet them. Robert searched the left-hand bank with a growing sense of excitement. And, suddenly, as the ship rounded the point of land he saw the famous city. A tangle of narrow streets lined with houses and large buildings seemed to flow down the sides of steep hills, all leading to the flat center of the city that faced the harbor. Above the jumble of buildings rose dozens of spires topped with crosses. Large buildings, one the Royal Palace, stood along the waterfront, separated from the water by a new-looking stone wharf, or quay. Between these buildings, and beyond the stone wall, Robert could see large, square, open spaces that were crowded with people.

Because of the importance of its passengers, the *Northampton* was directed to an anchorage near the foundation of the Royal Palace itself. Robert waited impatiently as the anchor was set and their passengers loaded into small boats and taken to the palace. When the ship was secure, his father was free to show the boy the city.

They climbed down the side of the ship and into a small boat which took them to a pier built out from the high wall of the quay. A short set of stairs led them upward through the wall and into a large square just to the east of the Royal Palace. They walked through a spotlessly clean market area. Some shops were meat markets where the skinned bodies of animals hung from the ceilings. Other shops contained fresh fish, lying in reed baskets and shielded from the sun by woven awnings. The walls of all of these shops were lined with glazed tiles.

"Lisbon is a beautiful city!" Robert said as he looked around him.

"This part of it is pretty," his father agreed as they walked down a narrow street along the back side of the Royal Palace. On both sides of the street the large buildings were made of shiny pink marble. "But you will see later that there is a great deal of poverty here. Perhaps one person out of ten in Lisbon does not have a house to live in and must sleep in the streets. Very few people other than the foreign merchants and members of the royal court have enough money to live comfortably."

They turned into a narrow, straight street and Robert noticed that they were walking up a slight slope. Most of the larger buildings they saw seemed to be churches or monasteries or convents. Men in the clothing of monks and friars walked through the streets everywhere.

"But if Portugal owns all of the gold mines in Brazil, why is the country so poor?" Robert asked, looking at a dirty, ragged beggar sitting on the steps of a nearby church.

"This beautiful country has a very foolish king," his father answered. "And his father, who died only five years ago, was even more foolish. They spent their wealth only on themselves and let their people have none of it. And, fortunately for us, they allow us foreigners—English, Dutch, French, and Swiss—to run their profit-making businesses. Except for the sale of food, the Portuguese merchants control almost nothing."

The houses alongside the street on which they walked had become steadily poorer as the path became steeper. As they climbed they had to walk carefully to avoid piles of garbage that had been thrown into the street. Soon they reached a small square and stopped to rest. As they looked back toward the harbor they could see the masts of their ship where it was anchored near the Royal Palace.

"Our passengers on this voyage are here to discuss an important agreement between the government of England and the Portuguese king. But they will not talk to the king. He takes no interest in the affairs of his country."

"But if the king does not run his country, who does?"

"Our passengers are here to talk with the Marquis de Pombal. He is the minister of foreign affairs for the king of Portugal. There are rumors that he controls the king himself. He certainly is the only man in the government who seems to have any ability."

They walked on up the hill until they reached its top. From there they could look out across the rooftops of the city. Robert counted seven hills from which the city spilled down into the harbor far below.

"It is so large!" he said in surprise. "It must be larger than London."

"No. Not larger than London." His father laughed. "Not one-third as large as London, I shouldn't think. Not more than 250,000 people.

"But it may be much older than London. Legend says that it was built by Ulysses the Greek, perhaps 1,000 years before the birth of Jesus. It was the capital of the Roman government here 100 years before Jesus' birth and 50 years before the Romans invaded England.

"The Moors occupied the country for centuries, until the Christian crusaders recaptured the city. Then Afonso I declared himself the first king of Portugal in 1147 and built the country and Lisbon into a world power."

He pointed to a cluster of low buildings standing to the east of the Royal Palace.

"Some of those buildings were built around 400 years ago. From the dock that stood there, Portuguese ships set out to explore the world. Nearly

300 years ago, in 1488, Dias sailed from here and discovered the passage around the southern end of Africa. And a few years after that, another Portuguese ship commanded by a man named Cabral discovered Brazil and its gold."

Intrigued by the strange smells and sights, the tall seaman and his son walked slowly down the steep, narrow street. Black slaves pushed heavily loaded carts through the narrow streets. Beggars cried out from the shadows of dozens of churches. Hooded monks moved through the crowds with an air of importance. Brown-skinned men offered them food from tiny shops tucked between large houses. They stopped in one shop so Captain Clarke could inspect the sailing equipment being offered for sale there.

"Christopher Columbus' brother Bartholomew owned a shop like this one," Captain Clarke told Robert. "I don't know exactly where it was, but in the late 1400's all of the port activities of Lisbon were in this part of the town. Christopher lived near here, too, I expect. His wife is buried in an old church nearby. As a young sailor only five or six years older than you are now, he sailed from Lisbon and explored the sea north of Iceland."

"Was that when he guessed that the world was round?" Robert asked.

His father laughed. "That was not Columbus' idea, son. Educated men had known that the earth was round for centuries before Columbus was born. They say that the ancient Greeks knew that the earth was a sphere.

"No thinking man of 300 years ago disagreed with Columbus' idea that he could reach India by sailing west. The only real question was how far west he would have to sail in order to reach India. The Portuguese seamen thought the world was much larger than Columbus did, and they were right. And so when Columbus, who was the captain of a Portuguese ship at the time, asked the king of Portugal to allow him to try to sail to India, he was refused—but not because the king believed the world was flat. Columbus had to go to the Spanish for money and ships because the Portuguese knew it would be less expensive if they could find a route to India around the southern tip of Africa. And Vasco da Gama did so, in 1498.

"But Lisbon did play a small part in Columbus' discovery of America. When he returned from his first voyage, a terrible storm caught them. His ship, the Nina, was separated from the other ships and took shelter in Lisbon harbor."

During the next week, Robert and his father roamed through the interesting city every day. They visited the shrines where images of the infant Jesus lay, and they were told amazing stories about these statues. One, they were told, often bled human blood, while the toenails of another grew so fast that they had to be trimmed weekly. Robert was surprised to see so many churches and other religious buildings. He asked his father how many there were.

"I don't think anyone has any idea how many churches, monasteries, and convents there are in

Lisbon. I certainly don't know. Hundreds, I suppose. Every large building that you saw from the top of the hill was either a palace or a religious building."

"The Roman Church is very strong here. This is the center of the Holy Inquisition in Portugal. Anyone who is accused of speaking against the Church may be tried and burned at the stake!"

Robert shuddered at the idea of being burned alive. His father continued to talk in a low voice.

"I told you the other day that the Marquis de Pombal has great influence with the king. He has tried for several years to destroy the Inquisition, but does not have enough power yet."

The next day they watched the city being decked out for the greatest celebration of the year—All Saints' Day. Fresh sand was spread on the streets and in the squares. Signboards had been repainted. Balconies and windows were hung with crimson drapes. Banners and flags flew from the dozens of religious buildings.

"I wish we could stay for the feast," Robert told his father the night before the celebration began.

"I wish we could too, son. But our business here is finished and we must leave with tomorrow morning's tide."

At five the next morning, Robert's father was busy preparing to leave the harbor. Sleepily Robert watched as the captain signed the papers required by the Portugal customs officials and then gave orders to raise the anchor. The ship began to move slowly away from the quay. Just then more than a hundred church bells began to ring, announcing the dawning of November first —All Saints' Day 1755.

The sky was clear in the early light. A small breeze from the northeast nudged the ship's sails and pushed them into the center of the harbor. Robert stood on the highest deck, feeling the soft breeze, listening to the pealing bells, and watching the people streaming through the streets toward the churches where they were to celebrate High Mass.

As the ship neared the center of the harbor, Robert felt the deck lurch suddenly under his feet.

"We're aground!" he heard a sailor shout as a loud *thump* boomed through the ship.

"Nonsense," Captain Clarke muttered as he moved quickly to the rail. "We have plenty of water here." But Robert could tell that his father was uncertain as to what made the ship lurch.

Now the entire ship was shivering. Men rushed along the decks and through hatches and doorways, searching for the cause of the strange motion. Robert looked into the water, expecting to see that they had struck some object—a sandbar perhaps, or a floating log. But the harbor water was calm and clear.

His searching look took his eyes back to the city they had just left. As he watched, the tower of one of the churches closest to the quay seemed to shudder for a moment and then slowly fell into the surrounding buildings. Then a wall of the Royal Palace collapsed into the square.

"Earthquake!" Robert heard his father shout. And the word was repeated again and again throughout the ship.

Orders were quickly given by the captain and passed on to the crew by the officers. Sailors scrambled into the rigging and unfurled sails flapped and rattled into place. Catching the wind, the *Northampton* hastily made her way across the bay and through the narrow channel into the open sea. Once the channel had been cleared and a course set, the captain again turned his attention to his son.

"An earthquake this near the shore may cause huge tidal waves," he explained. "It seems like a terrible thing to leave those unfortunate people behind. But there is little we can do to help them now. A captain must always think of his ship and its passengers first. If we had been caught in the harbor by a tidal wave, the *Northampton* would surely have been destroyed."

The wave caused by the earthquake caught the *Northampton* an hour later. But the ship was in deep water and the men on board hardly noticed its passing. The merchant ship, its crew, and its passengers escaped without damage.

But in Lisbon the damage was terrible. Most of the people in the city were in the churches and convents, celebrating the All Saints' Day Mass. The tall steeples were the first structures to fall and many of them fell through the roofs and onto the worshipping people inside. Then the walls of the larger buildings fell into the streets, killing hundreds of people who had managed to escape from the ruined churches.

The first shocks were sudden and sharp. A roar, like underground thunder, drowned out the screams of the frightened and injured people. Clouds of dust hid the sun as the shaking became slower and much more violent. After a minute or two the side-to-side shaking of the earth changed to an up-and-down motion. Like a cracking whip, the earth rippled in waves that shattered the foundations of all of the buildings that had stood near the quay.

Ten long minutes later, the earth again became still. Survivors rushed into the squares, only to find them filled with debris. Hoping that there would be ships to take them away, thousands rushed to the stone quay along the waterfront. But, as they crowded the wall, the ground again began to shake. The soft earth under the quay shifted and the foundation broke. The stone wall that had seemed so safe and solid cascaded into the harbor, carrying with it hundreds of people.

Fires started almost immediately. The thousands of altar candles that had been lighted in honor of All Saints' Day had set fire to the tapestries that had hung in every church. Open cooking fires in the houses spilled out of their hearths and set fire to the wooden floors. Wherever fires started, they swept through the ruins unchecked. The few people who were interested in fighting the fires found no water available and the streets impassable because of the rubble. Fanned by the growing

An engraving shows Lisbon in 1755 being swept away by a tsunami, or sea wave, probably caused by an underwater earthquake. In one day, the old city of Lisbon was destroyed by tremors, fire,

and finally by a wall of water, higher than a two-story building, that washed a half a mile inland.

wind, the fires raged for days before they burned themselves out.

Only an hour after the first shocks, a second series of tremors smashed through the ruined town. More walls fell, but few of the survivors were killed. Then almost immediately the entire bay seemed to drain nearly dry. Rocks that had never been seen before stood dry a mile or more from the shore. Hundreds of people stopped their searching through the debris to stare at this strange sight.

Then they heard a dull roaring sound. At first they feared that the earthquake was starting again. But it was something even more terrible.

A wall of water, higher than a two-story building, was rushing up the bay toward them. This was what Captain Clarke had called "the tidal wave." Now the Japanese name *tsunami* is used, since the wave has nothing to do with the tides. It is apparently caused by the sudden shifting of the ocean bottom during underwater earthquakes. The waves are quite small in the open sea but grow as they pass through shallow water. This tsunami smashed into the ruined harbor at a speed of several hundred miles-an-hour, and carrying more people to their deaths, it washed a half a mile inland.

At noon another series of sharp shocks struck the city. But there was nothing left to destroy. Thirty-two churches and 53 palace buildings lay in total ruin. Of the 20,000 houses that had made up the city, only 3,000 that had stood on the more distant hills remained upright and even these were badly damaged. In the rubble lay the bodies of 15,000 people and many more floated in the now-calm water of the bay or in the Atlantic Ocean many miles away.

The king and his family had escaped without injury. When the first shock struck, the entire court was on the road between Belem Tower and Lisbon. Safely away from the falling buildings, the king and his followers were only frightened by the earthquake.

But the king did not know what to do. "Return to Lisbon," some of his advisors said. "Take your court and family to safety in Belem Tower," other advisors suggested. "Pray to God for forgiveness and protection," he was told by others. Confused and frightened and unable to make a decision, the poor king could do nothing.

At that moment a lone rider galloped into the cluster of carriages. It was the Marquis de Pombal, the king's minister of foreign affairs and his chief advisor. Unhurt by the earthquake and knowing that the royal court was moving to Belem Tower, Pombal had leaped on a horse and had ridden after them. As he slid to the ground, the king turned to him.

"Pombal! Thank God you are here! What can be done? What can be done?"

Pombal was breathing hard after his rapid ride. But he answered the king calmly. "Sire!" He bowed his head a little, then looked at the king. "We must bury the dead and feed the living."

This simple answer impressed the king a great deal. He immediately gave Pombal the power to do whatever was necessary, and took his followers on to Belem Tower.

Pombal immediately returned to Lisbon and took command. Using the power that the king had given him, he took control of all of the important parts of the government and ran Portugal for the next 20 years. Under his leadership, Portugal again became an important country in the world.

When he arrived in Lisbon, Pombal found no trace of streets or squares anywhere along the waterfront. The entire center of the city was nothing but a pile of rubble. For the next three days he lived in a carriage, sleeping, eating, and giving orders as he moved from place to place. He ordered the army to surround the city. He posted armed guards near the Royal Treasury and along the streets to stop looting. He directed teams of men to begin clearing the debris from the streets. He ordered fresh water and food to be brought in, and began the rebuilding of kitchens and ovens so that the workers could be fed.

One major problem was how to bury the 15,000 bodies that were taken from the rubble. He knew that he must dispose of the corpses before disease broke out. Over the violent objections of the church officials, he loaded the bodies into old barges, sailed these down the river, and sank them in the Atlantic Ocean.

Within a week, during which time Pombal ordered the execution of dozens of looters, the job of rebuilding the city was organized and under way. Pombal then turned his attention to another important matter. He began a careful study of the damage done by the quake. He talked to people about their experiences to gather information about the length of time each shock lasted and the effects of the quake on the ocean. He toured far inland, noticing where the earthquake had cracked the earth and in which direction these fissures ran. He also studied the damage done to various types of buildings in and around Lisbon. To help with this work, the Japanese emperor sent a team of builders. This was perhaps the first scientific study of an earthquake, and the information Pombal gathered helped him to build a new city that was much more resistant to earthquake shocks.

Geologists, scientists who study the earth, can only guess at how strong the Lisbon earthquake was since it occurred many, many years before the invention of instruments that measure earthquake shocks. It certainly was not the strongest earthquake in history, but it affected a large part of the world.

The shocks themselves were felt, or their results were seen, over nearly one-third of Europe. In England, more than 1,000 miles away from Lisbon, a fissure opened up in a field and plaster was shaken from at least one house. Across the English Channel, in the Netherlands, water in canals and rivers was set into such violent motion by the shocks that buoys and ships broke loose from their chains. In a part of what is now Czechoslovakia, nearly 1,400 miles away from the center, or *focus*, of the quake, a warm spring became muddy and then stopped flowing. For a thousand miles in all directions the chandeliers of the churches in which All Saints' Day Mass was being celebrated began to jiggle and swing as the shocks passed through the stone buildings. These shocks did little damage outside of Portugal but were felt over more than a million square miles of the earth's surface.

It was the sea waves that did the most damage to places other than Lisbon. The tsunami rushed out into the Atlantic at speeds of about 500 miles-an-hour. Along the coast of Morocco, the waves built up to what must have been nearly 50 feet high and swept away 10,000 people who lived along the edge of the sea. To the north, the waves curved up the coast and reached England in about five hours, but did little damage.

No one in England was killed by the earthquake or its aftereffects, but the cause of the disaster was the topic of heated discussion and bitter debate in that country. Was the crushing of Lisbon the "wrath of God," or did the earthquake have a natural cause? This was the important question of 18th Century England.

During the previous century, between 1642 and 1688, England had been torn by a civil war between Catholics and Protestants, a conflict that continues in parts of Ireland even today. Sickened by these years of war over religion, many people turned away from all religion. Going to church on

Sunday had become less and less popular. Going to plays and gambling, both of which were frowned upon by many Protestant ministers, became popular forms of entertainment.

At about the same time, experimental science began to develop and the followers of the so-called "New Philosophy" were able to explain many of the workings of nature.

The evangelists of new religions, such as John Wesley, continually warned the people that God would punish them for their sins. They tried to win new converts by explaining every catastrophe as being the "wrath of God." A disease that killed large numbers of cows, a plague of locusts, an unusual display of Northern Lights, or even a thunderstorm was used to frighten people back into the church.

On February 8, 1750, a mild earthquake struck the British Isles. No one at that time had any idea as to the real cause of earthquakes and many attempts were made to explain this one in natural terms. Some of the early scientists suggested that Jupiter was too close to the earth. Others pointed out that the pressure of the air was very low just before the quake. Still others thought that the newly discovered electricity in the air caused the earth to shake.

Exactly one month later, on March eighth, a second earthquake was felt. Again little damage was done and no one was killed. But John Wesley told his followers that it was a "second warning from God" and predicted that a third, more violent earthquake would occur on April eighth and kill all of the sinners in London.

Thousands of people flocked back to the churches to repent. Thousands of others left London to find safety in less inhabited areas. Some even bought pills that were advertised as being "very good against the earthquake."

Unfortunately for John Wesley's cause, nothing happened on April eighth, and many of the recent converts returned to their gambling and play-going. But the Lisbon earthquake five years later gave the followers of Wesley another chance. Lisbon, they said, was destroyed because its people were wicked. And so the arguments began again. The scientists were not able to offer any better explanations than they had before, and could do nothing but state their belief that earthquakes were natural phenomena that someday would be understood. On the other hand, the evangelists could not explain why, out of all the wicked cities in the world, Lisbon had been selected to be smashed.

And the debate continued until, many years later, scientists began to find some of the answers to the question of why the solid earth suddenly begins to shake. The question is still not fully answered.

CHAPTER THREE

NEW MADRID, MISSOURI DECEMBER, 1811 - MARCH, 1812

WHERE ARE EARTHQUAKES likely to occur? If we were to put a dot on a map of the world showing the locations of all of the earthquakes that have occurred during the history of man we would see a very interesting pattern. Nearly 95 percent of all the earthquakes that we know about have taken place in two narrow belts.

One of these belts nearly circles the Pacific Ocean. From the islands of New Zealand, this earthquake pattern passes in an arc to the northern side of Australia. It then turns north to sweep across the islands of Indonesia and the Philip-

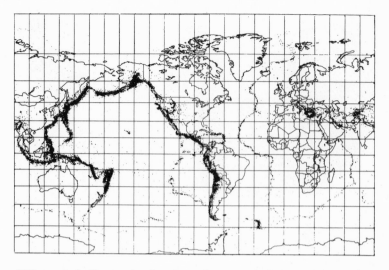

This map indicates the location of many of the earthquakes that occurred during the period 1961–1969. There are two main earthquake belts—one circles the Pacific Ocean, and a second starts at the Philippines and crosses Asia and Europe to Spain. A third, less distinct, belt is the Mid-Atlantic Ridge.

pines. From there it goes to Japan and to Alaska. Turning south, it follows the west coast of North America and the west coast of South America. A branch of this belt includes the islands at the mouth of the Caribbean Sea. If you look at a relief map of the world, you will see that this Pacific earthquake belt is about the same as the pattern of high mountain ranges that also circles the Pacific Ocean.

The second earthquake belt also follows mountain ranges. It touches the Pacific belt at the Philippines and goes across Asia and Europe. It passes through the Himalaya Mountains, the Caucasus Mountains between the Caspian Sea and the Black Sea, and through the Alps to Portugal. If you have studied volcanoes, you may realize

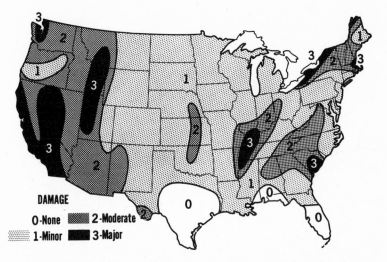

DAMAGE

0-None 2-Moderate

1-Minor 3-Major

This earthquake risk map divides the United States into four zones: Zone 0, areas where no earthquake damage is expected; Zone 1, expected minor damage; Zone 2, expected moderate damage; and Zone 3, where major destructive earthquakes may occur.

that these two earthquake belts are roughly the same as the belts where volcanoes usually occur.

Most of the earthquakes that you will read about in this book took place within one or the other of these two belts. But earthquakes have occurred in other parts of the world.

We expect strong earthquakes in mountainous areas that border on deep bodies of water. So, the type of area where we would least expect a violent earthquake would be a low river valley near the center of a large continent. Yet it was in just such an area that one of the strongest earthquakes in the earth's history actually did occur.

If we look at a map of southeastern Missouri we will find, tucked into a bend of the Mississippi River, the little town of New Madrid.

The land here is flat. The nearest tall mountains are hundreds of miles away. The soil of the river valley is very rich, made of deep, dark mud and clay dropped by the flooding water of the Mississippi. Under it lies a layer of sand that is always full of water that has seeped into it from the river.

About 3,000 people live in the town of New Madrid now, and perhaps 50,000 people live nearby. But in the early 1800's the area had just begun to be settled. A part of the Louisiana Purchase, Missouri had been sold to the United States by Napoleon in 1803. The territory had not yet been admitted to the Union as a state, and Indians often still made bloody raids on little communities such as New Madrid.

In the year 1811 only about 800 people lived in New Madrid. The town was made up of 18 streets leading down to the river and ten streets crossing these and paralleling the river. All of the buildings were one-story log cabins. Outside of the town limits were a few cabins built by farmers.

The night of December 15, 1811, was clear but cold and the people living in the cabins along the banks of the Mississippi River were in bed early. Shortly after two o'clock the next morning, when they were all sound asleep, they were awakened by strange sounds. The log walls of their houses seemed to be groaning, creaking, and popping. As they lay there, listening, they felt the ground begin to shake.

Quickly gathering up warm clothing and blankets, everyone in New Madrid rushed out into the cold night. Stone chimneys began to sway and then to fall. Clouds of dust billowed up into the sky. Some people thought that they saw bolts of lightning in the dust clouds.

The shaking grew stronger until even the log houses themselves began to collapse. Then the shocks became weak and almost disappeared. As the cold, frightened people tried to go back into houses that were still standing, the shaking started again and they had to return to the open. They huddled together to draw warmth and courage from each other. At dawn, they stirred themselves and looked at what had been their homes. As they walked through the streets, littered with fallen rocks and logs, another earthquake began. This one proved to be at least as strong as the first, and more houses collapsed.

Very few people in New Madrid were injured by the two earthquakes. This is because they were not in tall buildings that could collapse and trap them. But nearly all of the log houses in the town had been destroyed or badly damaged. From this fact, today's geologists have guessed that the town must have stood at the *epicenter* of the earthquake. This is the point on the earth's surface that is directly above the earthquake's *focus,* or source. They know that the shaking of the earth under New Madrid must have been very, very strong because houses made of logs are rarely damaged by earthquakes.

The almost total destruction of New Madrid makes this unusually located earthquake interesting. But what is even more unusual is the fact that this quake was felt over an area at least as large as the earthquake that struck Lisbon. Canadians felt the shaking of the earth. People in New Orleans reported the first two shocks. Boston was shaken. In Charleston, South Carolina, a bell began to ring as the spire of St. Philip's Church swayed in time with the shivering earth. All up and down the eastern coast, pendulum clocks stopped as they were thrown out of time by the shaking. Perhaps over a million miles of the earth's surface, people felt the earth tremble.

The earthquake that destroyed New Madrid also changed the countryside around there. Along this stretch of the Mississippi River high bluffs stood along the waterfront. Many of these slipped into the muddy water as the shocks hit them. Several streets of New Madrid that ran close to the river were carried away by collapsing banks.

The water of the Mississippi and of several tributaries was whipped into heavy waves by the shaking of the riverbed and by the collapsing banks. Large waves dashed up and down the river, swamping small boats and damaging many buildings that stood near the shore. In one section, many trees were uprooted by these waves. One steamer captain reported that the Mississippi River actually flowed backward for a while!

Huge splits in the earth, some ten feet wide and four and one-half feet deep, opened up in the soft, water-deposited soil. Most of these fissures closed up almost at once. This apparently put pressure on the water-soaked sand layer below and water was thrown violently up to the surface. These "blows" were made of water, sand, and air. The damp sand was blown ten to 15 feet into the air while the air that had been trapped beneath the earth escaped with a roar and a whistle. In places, the sand was spread over wide areas of farmland and was many feet deep. This thick layer of sand made farming these areas almost impossible for many years.

Many miles to the east, in Kentucky, James Audubon, the famous naturalist, was riding a horse when the second earthquake struck. He later wrote that "the ground waved like a field of corn before the breeze."

As a result of all this shaking, a large mass of land—perhaps 30,000 square miles—sank between five and 15 feet. You can still see the scars of this sinking. Twenty square miles of western Tennessee sank so low that the hollow filled with water. This area is now called Reelfoot Lake. The trees that had grown on this once-level plain were killed by the water. Marshes and swamps formed in other sunken areas. In all, more than 200 square miles of forests were killed. It was reported that a man could paddle his canoe through the branches of walnuts, oaks, mulberrys, and cypress trees that had once stood on high, dry ground. Today thousands of stumps can be seen in these bodies of water.

Most of these changes came about suddenly, during the morning of December 16. But the

Reelfoot Lake was formed by the New Madrid earthquake. The forest land sank so low that water filled in the hollow.

earthquakes were not finished. Several times a day for the next year the earth around New Madrid was shaken. These were mostly small quakes, although on January 23 and again on February seventh, shocks as strong as the first two smashed through the region.

Many people tried to keep track of how many shocks they could feel. A Dr. Robertson, living a hundred miles up the Mississippi River from New Madrid, counted 500 and then stopped when he grew tired of the game. In fact, as the shivering of the ground became less and less strong, most people grew bored with the whole thing and went about their business without noticing the shocks.

But one man did not. Mr. Jared Brooks lived in Louisville, Kentucky, and became fascinated by the shocks that he could feel every few hours. Between December 16 and March 15, when the shocks became almost too weak to feel, Brooks counted a total of 1,874!

Soon after he began keeping count, Brooks tried to find some way to detect the little shocks —the ones he could not feel. He had noticed that his pendulum clock had stopped during the worst of the shocks. It occurred to him that perhaps a pendulum might help him with his problem. Over the next few months he experimented with pendulums of different lengths. He also made several devices that contained heavy weights held by weak springs. He found these would vibrate as the earth shook even when the shaking was so gentle that he could not feel it himself.

This may have been the first time anyone in the United States attempted to study earthquake shocks with instruments. But it was far from being the first attempt to do so. Nearly 2,000 years ago a Chinese astronomer named Chang Heng built a simple *seismograph,* as such instruments are called. No one can be certain that Chang's device worked, but it certainly was an artistic attempt. Chang made a bronze jar with a copper dome about three feet across. Eight brass dragon heads were spaced around the outside of the dome. Into the open mouth of each dragon Chang placed a brass ball and connected to the dome, inside the jar, he placed a pendulum. The idea of this device was that when an earthquake shock struck the dome, the pendulum would begin to swing in the same direction as the shock was traveling. The movement of the pendulum would then cause a ball to be dropped into the mouth of a brass frog that crouched on the ground below each dragon head.

As strange as this instrument seems to us, Chang was on the right track. A pendulum is nothing but a weight hanging from something that is tightly attached to a solid object. If the solid object moves, the weight on the end of the pendulum tends to remain still. You can prove this to yourself. Hang a heavy weight from a long string and hold the string by the end opposite from the weight. With a little practice you should be able to move your hand rapidly back and forth without moving the weight very much.

This seismographic recording indicates earthquake tremors or shocks. Note the variation in the waves.

This weight that remained still as the earth moved around it was what scientists were looking for. From the time of Chang Heng, pendulums were used in almost all seismographs. But the early ones were not sensitive enough. Before 1880 the seismograph pendulums were attached to pens that drew lines on a moving piece of paper. In an attempt to make these instruments more sensitive, the weights became larger and larger, one finally reaching the tremendous size of more than 20 tons!

But during the last 100 years several better ways to record the movement of the earth beneath a seismograph have been found. Beams of light shining on photographic paper were tried. Electric currents, generated by the shaking earth acting on magnets, were also used. Electric eyes are used in some modern seismographs, while others use magnetic tape.

Many different types of seismographs are now used, each built to detect a different type of earthquake shock. Even the slightest shock such as the touch of a feather or the crawling of a nearby spider will be recorded by these instruments. By studying these records, geologists can tell many things about an earthquake, even though its focus may be many thousands of miles away.

The first thing that can be learned from the seismograph record is how far away from the instrument the earthquake was. If this information can be collected from at least three different stations, the location of the earthquake can be found. Suppose the instrument at Seismograph Station A indicates that the earthquake was 1,000 miles away. The scientists draw a circle on a map using Station A as the center. If the scale on the map is three inches equals 1,000 miles, they will make the radius of the circle three inches. This way, every point on the circle is 1,000 miles away from Station A. Seismograph Station B reports that the earthquake was located 500 miles away from it. A second circle, this one 500 miles around Station B, is drawn on the map. This circle crosses the first circle in two places. A third report from Seismograph Station C will allow the scientists to draw a third circle on their map. This circle will cross through one of the two intersections of the other

This illustration shows a way scientists can locate an earthquake's epicenter, the surface directly above the earthquake's underground source. Seismographs around the world record a shock and how far away it is from each station, but these measuring instruments do not give the quake's exact location. Scientists can draw a circle from each station on a map; each circle represents the distance recorded at a specific station. Where the circles intercept, or cross, is the exact location of the epicenter.

circles. Where all three circles cross is the location of the earthquake.

These circles tell the scientists where *on the surface* of the earth the effect of the quake was felt. This spot is called the epicenter of the earthquake. From the seismograph records the scientists can also get some idea how far *beneath the surface* the actual slipping of the rocks took place. This spot, where the rocks broke and slipped, is called the focus of the earthquake. Both bits of information are important. A deep earthquake may not do much damage at the epicenter but may be felt over many square miles of the earth's surface. A shallow quake, on the other hand, may do a great deal of damage at the epicenter but go unnoticed only a few miles away.

The seismograph record also gives some information as to the strength of the earthquake. This, when added to the information as to the exact location of the quake and its depth, allows the scientists to guess what damage was done long before any information can be sent out of a city hit by the earthquake. It also allows them to predict whether or not the earthquake will produce a sea wave that may cause damage to seashore areas on the other side of the earth. Knowing whether a tsunami will form makes it possible to save many lives.

Scientists still have a great deal to learn about earthquakes and about the center of the earth. But with accurate, sensitive instruments such as the modern seismograph they are learning more each day. Perhaps someday they will be able to predict where an earthquake will take place and how strong it will be.

CHAPTER FOUR

SAN FRANCISCO 1906

POLICE SERGEANT JESSE COOK looked at his watch. It was 12 minutes after five o'clock. His beat was the fruit and vegetable market of San Francisco and it was busy this time of morning. Nearby farmers had brought their produce by horse-drawn wagons and were getting their goods ready to sell to early shoppers.

As he stood on the corner of Washington and Davis Streets, chatting with a friend, Sergeant Cook noticed the sudden restlessness of the horses. It was followed immediately by a deep rumbling sound that seemed to come out of the earth. He looked up Washington Street and saw the brick surface of the street rippling. He later remembered, "It was as if the waves of the ocean were coming toward me, and billowing as they came."

In another part of town, newspaper editor John Barrett and some of his co-workers had just finished work. They were standing on the sidewalk waiting for an early morning trolley car. Suddenly they found themselves staggering as the earth beneath their feet moved rapidly. The next thing they knew, they were lying on the ground. They tried to get up but couldn't. Barrett saw the buildings around him sway and the trolley tracks twist in the street. Electric wires broke and were "wriggling like serpents, flashing blue sparks all the time." There were gashes in the streets and water from broken pipes sprayed like giant fountains into the air. They noticed the smell of leaking gas.

The first low, growling, unseen rumble changed to a roar made up of the jangling of broken glass, the grinding of stone against stone, and the splintering of wooden buildings.

On a hill overlooking San Francisco, a surprised Bailey Millard sat amid his scattered easel, canvas, paints, and brushes. He had started the day trying to capture on canvas the way San Francisco looked when the sun first touched its buildings.

He watched buildings collapse in the city below. Seven million dollars' worth of stone and bricks was shaken off of City Hall. Its framework remained standing, like the bones of an upright skeleton.

All of this happened in only 65 to 75 seconds. It seemed like an eternity to those who felt it.

People all over town were rudely awakened. Many ran out into the streets in their night clothes, or less, when they realized what was happening. Some were pinned beneath the wreckage of their houses and were rescued later. Others were killed by falling beams and bricks. Everywhere, people were dazed and confused.

San Francisco had suffered other earthquakes. But most of them had been only slightly felt, if at all. Almost 100 years before, in 1808, an earthquake was reported in the area but there weren't many people to feel it. There was a large one in 1836, and another in 1838.

In 1848 gold was discovered in California and people rushed to that sparsely settled part of the country in hopes of finding riches. San Francisco soon became a booming city with buildings being thrown together hastily to house the newcomers. The population grew from 2,000 to 20,000 in just one year. By 1900 there were more than 340,000, and two years later it was estimated there were 485,000 people living there.

Minor earthquakes were felt regularly and were mostly ignored. There were larger ones that caused damage to buildings, but rarely was anyone killed. The big killer was fire.

The combination of flimsy wooden buildings and the stiff breezes that whipped around San

*Devastated San Francisco
after the 1906 earthquake and fires.*

Francisco's hills made uncontrollable fires difficult to prevent. Fire fighters and fire fighting equipment became important to the city. And soon builders were paying more attention to whether or not building materials were fireproof.

The sumptuous Palace Hotel was built to withstand both fire and earthquake. Its foundation rested on cement pillars that were buried 12 feet into the ground. Its two-foot-thick brick walls were strengthened by 3,000 tons of reinforced iron strips. Surely no earthquake could damage such a building.

To guard against fire, there were water storage tanks on the hotel roof and in the basement. Even if the city water supply should fail, the Palace would have its own water. In addition to its regular pipes for bathrooms and kitchens, there were five *miles* of water pipe to carry water for fire fighting. There were 350 faucets that were connected to 20,000 feet of fire hose. In each of the 800 hotel rooms there was a heat-sensitive instrument that would automatically sound a fire alarm if the room became too hot. And as if that were not enough, every floor was checked every half hour by watchmen who had to push buttons along the way to signal that everything was all right. If one failed to push any button, the office would assume something was wrong.

The Palace had several fires in the 31 years before the 1906 earthquake, but all were brought quickly under control. The building was considered to be fireproof and earthquake-proof.

San Francisco was a very lively city. Many fortunes were made there, and people were anxious to spend their money. The theater flourished and even New York's Metropolitan Opera Company brought performances to this west coast city. The night before the big earthquake, a world-famous singer performed for the people of San Francisco. The singer's name was Enrico Caruso. He was from Italy.

Just the week before, the papers were full of the news of the eruption of Mt. Vesuvius, in Caruso's homeland. It was said that lava ran in rivers down the mountainside and burned villages as it went. The generous people of San Francisco had collected $23,000 to send to the Italians who were left homeless because of the disaster. The reporters asked Caruso why people kept rebuilding villages around the mountain which erupted regularly. He had no answer.

When the jolts from the earthquake awakened Caruso on the morning of April 18, he was afraid it might have damaged his voice. So he ran to the window, opened it, and sounded a magnificent note to the startled people who had run into the street below. He was badly frightened by the earthquake and vowed never to return to San Francisco. He kept that promise.

Nearly 50 fires were reported in downtown San Francisco before 5:30 that morning. Some were caused by fire thrown into the room from a fireplace. Others were from cooking stoves that were knocked over by the shocks. One that was par-

These tracks in San Francisco buckled during the 1906 earthquake.

One tall house leans on its neighbor that seems not to have been affected by the 1906 earthquake.

ticularly disastrous was caused when someone lit a fire to cook breakfast. The stove was connected to a chimney that had been blocked by the earthquake, and sparks caused the wall to catch fire. This "Ham and Eggs Fire," as it came to be called, was responsible for the burning of a large section of San Francisco.

All of these fires could probably have been controlled, but the water mains that brought water to the city were broken. Firemen who connected their hoses to fire hydrants found only a small trickle of water which quickly dwindled to nothing. They tried other hydrants, but with the same results. How could they fight fire without water?

In the Italian section of town, many people broke open vats of homemade wine and vinegar to pour on the flames. A few people had water storage tanks on their roofs. When the fire raged out of control and threatened the whole city, the firemen decided to level an area between the fire and the rest of the city with dynamite. But none of this worked. The fires continued to burn.

People whose homes had been damaged only slightly by the earthquake saw them go up in flames. The parks were full of people with no homes and only a few belongings that they were able to carry. Families became separated. For days children and parents wandered through the city looking for each other.

Widow Hazel Yardley had slipped out of the house at five o'clock the morning of the earthquake. She was headed for the produce market when the quake threw her to the ground. When she was able to get up she ran in panic back home, where she had left her two-year-old Annie sleeping.

The house was completely demolished. The woman dug hysterically through the ruins but she couldn't find Annie. Neighbors told her no one could have lived through such destruction, and they led her away from the rubble. She had found a small picture of Annie that she clutched to her.

Hazel Yardley refused to believe that Annie was dead. She wandered through the streets, stopping everyone she saw. Had they seen the little girl in the picture? Always, the answer was the same, "No."

Two days later a policeman took the woman to the Ferry Building and she was put on a boat for Oakland, across the bay. Many children who were alone had been sent across the bay. She searched the face of each child she saw. Every adult was shown the picture. But there was no word of Annie.

By this time Oakland had received 50,000 people who had no homes. There were refugee camps set up for them in various parts of town. Mrs. Yardley steadfastly walked through one camp after another, still searching.

It was after dark when she reached the camp of tents where Harry Adams and his family were sheltered. Adams and his wife were sitting outside their tent, breaking bread into a pot of stew. Mrs.

Yardley went up to them and showed her picture and asked her question again.

Mr. Adams got up and went into the tent. He returned with Annie in his arms.

He had rescued her when the house collapsed. Seeing no parent around, he took her with his wife and their two children to safety.

A joyous Mrs. Yardley knelt and gave thanks to God as she hugged Annie to her.

Telephone communications from San Francisco to the outside world were cut off by the earthquake. Telegraph lines went with the fire. The rest of the world was left to guess about the fate of San Francisco, and wild rumors spread about how many had been killed. People living in New York, Chicago, London, Paris, Berlin, and Tokyo read about the raging fire (which was true), about soldiers killing people who were suspected of stealing (which was partly true), and about people dying of starvation (which was not true).

People left the city by ferryboat and by train. The Southern Pacific railroad moved 70 passengers out of the city every minute, eventually taking 300,000 people away from San Francisco. There was no charge for this train trip. The railroad company also shipped into the city 37,000 tons of relief supplies.

The Army, commanded by Brigadier General Frederick Funston, moved in immediately to help keep order. General Funston gave orders that were backed by the mayor to shoot anyone caught stealing. This practice was later severely criticized by the public, and it is difficult now to know how many people were actually killed this way. The general claimed only three cases were reported to him. But there were reports of dozens who were shot. The stories were exaggerated, but no one knows how much.

The Marines and Navy arrived on Thursday, a little more than 24 hours after the earthquake. The fires were still raging. They docked fire-boats, hospital boats, and boats carrying fresh water and supplies at the city's piers. They brought more explosives to use in blasting a clear path between the blazing fire and what was left of the city.

For the next 48 hours the fire fighting continued. Several times fires in one section of town would seem to be under control but a fresh wind would whip the embers into flames and leap across dynamited paths to devour another section of town. Firemen worked until they dropped from exhaustion. When one fell, a volunteer would take his place. Finally everything except the waterfront area was under control.

Fire teams concentrated their efforts on that part of town. Inch by inch they gained ground and eventually, on Saturday morning, April 21, the fire was over. Three days before, it had all started. Now it began to rain. Exhausted, sleep-hungry, dazed people cheered.

Even before the fire was out, city officials and a group of citizens had formed a committee to see to the needs of the people. Congress had voted emergency funds for food, clothing, medical supplies, and shelter.

In looking over the damaged city, it was discovered that 4.7 square miles of land and 28,000 buildings had burned. This included the Palace Hotel. It was estimated that more than 600 people died from this earthquake. But not all of these people were in San Francisco.

Eighty-seven were patients at Agnews State Insane Asylum near San Jose. Along with them died 11 nurses, the superintendent of the hospital, and his wife. In the city of San Jose, 21 people died. A sawmill at Hinckley Gulch was buried along with nine workers by a landslide.

The earthquake that caused all of this damage left signs along a path that was 200 miles long. This path lies over what is known as the San Andreas Fault. The San Andreas Fault is not just one big crack in the earth down the coast of California. It is a lot of parallel breaks in the surface of the earth—breaks that lie directly over a section of the earth's surface that is under much strain. Scientists think of it as a place where huge pieces of the crust of the earth rub and grind past each other very slowly. Sometimes pressures inside the earth cause these sections to move past each other smoothly and only cause small quakes. At other times these pieces fit together so tightly that they do not move easily. However, the pressure that causes the movement is still there and it builds up. The pressure may even cause the crust to

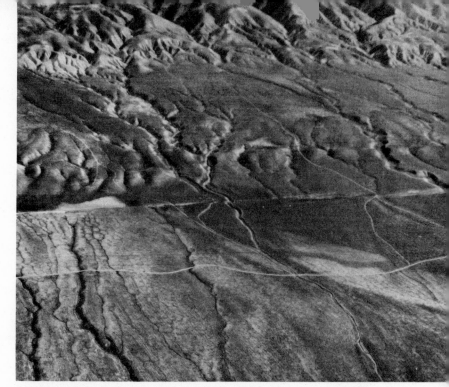

In this aerial view of the San Andreas Fault, the line across the center of the photograph traces a break in the earth's surface. This break lies directly over a section of the earth that is under great strain.

"bend" out of shape a little. When the pressure becomes great enough, the sections will finally move past each other, only now with great force. It has been estimated that the shock waves from this huge build-up of energy in 1906 traveled at two miles-per-second.

At one place along the California coast, where the earthquake traveled under the ocean, its shock was felt by a ship. The *Argo* must have been directly above the fault, because it was as if the ship had been blasted with an explosive. Some of the steel plate of her body buckled. Bolts were blown out of place. Her captain later remembered that for a few seconds, "the whole ship appeared to be breaking up—and in a perfectly calm sea!"

At sea, 150 miles due west of San Francisco, the schooner *John A. Campbell* rose high in the water, hesitated a moment, and then smashed downward again. The sleeping crew jumped from their bunks to see what had happened. When they were on deck, they could see nothing out of the ordinary. It was as if they had all had the same bad dream at once. The captain wrote in the log, "Sudden motion, unexplained. The shock felt as if the vessel struck . . . and then appeared to drag over soft ground." But of course, it could not have dragged soft ground—the ocean bottom was more than 14,000 feet below. It was only later that the captain discovered they had felt the shocks of the earthquake that had ripped up the coast of California.

The shock of the restless movement of the earth's crust plowed a furrow across fields, through barns, over hills, and down stream beds. In many places there were no deaths only because there were no people living there. It demolished whole forests of redwood trees, sent tons of coastline rocks into the sea, and re-routed the flow of water in creek beds.

All of the effects of the earthquake were not bad. Scientists from the University of California studied the quake and published their findings. This study is thought by some people to be one of the greatest contributions to modern seismology (the study of earthquakes). Up until this time it was generally believed that earthquakes resulted in rocks slipping vertically, leaving one side of a fault higher than the other.

Measurements made along the San Andreas Fault, however, showed that most of the movement was horizontal. Creek beds, roads, and fences that had lain along a straight line now jogged as much as 15 to 20 feet out of line. This idea of horizontal movement was so new that scientists found it hard to believe. In fact, they were hesitant to even discuss it. Those who did, suggested it was a freak occurrence, and not what normally happens. We know today that many faults have more movement in a horizontal direction than they do in a vertical direction.

Earthquakes are measured in two ways. One measure is of the energy that comes from the source of the earthquake. This amount of energy is called the *magnitude* of the quake. Seismographs record information that allows scientists to calculate the magnitude.

The other measurement of an earthquake has to do with how much it is felt and how much damage is done. This is called the *intensity* of an earthquake. Intensity is usually measured by the observations of people who were in the area. These observations are described according to the Modified Mercalli Scale, which is divided into 12 parts, as follows:

I. A shock recorded by seismographs only. Not noticed by people, although they may feel dizzy or nauseated. Sometimes birds and other animals seem uneasy.

II. A shock felt indoors by a few people, especially if they are on the higher floors of a tall building. Hanging objects and tree limbs may sway.

III. This shock is felt by a number of people on lower as well as upper levels of buildings. Automobiles that are standing still may rock slightly.

IV. Many people indoors feel this shock, and a few who are outside. Doors, windows, and dishes may rattle.

V. Almost everyone indoors, even those who were sleeping, may feel this one. Pictures may fall off walls, bells in churches may ring, and furniture may shift slightly.

VI. Everyone, indoors and outdoors, will feel this one. Poorly constructed buildings may be damaged. Furniture may overturn. Windows may break.

VII. People are frightened and run outside. They find it difficult to stand. Drivers of automobiles cannot control the movement of the cars. Well constructed buildings are not damaged, but ordinary buildings suffer some damage. Bricks and stones are dislodged.

VIII. Most chimneys fall. People are alarmed and may panic. Trees shake with some breaking off. Damage to well constructed buildings is slight; ordinary buildings may collapse.

IX. Total destruction of a few buildings. People are generally panic-stricken. There are cracks in the ground. Underground pipes sometimes break.

X. Ground cracks may be several inches wide. Well built wooden buildings and bridges are badly damaged. Cement and asphalt roads may develop open cracks.

XI. Stone buildings are destroyed. Bridges fall, and railway lines are twisted. Pipes buried in the earth are all broken.

XII. Damage is complete. All manmade structures are destroyed. There are great changes in the surface of the earth.

This scale was first set up in 1902 by an Italian seismologist whose name was Mercalli. It was brought up to date in 1931 by two Americans to include such modern things as tall buildings and automobiles. When you use a Mercalli number, it is always written in Roman numerals. It measures intensity, which is determined by people's senses.

The other measurement we mentioned, magnitude, is first taken from a seismograph. This measurement is then adjusted, depending on how far the instrument is from the source of the earthquake.

The strength of the quake is expressed in numbers on a scale called the Richter Scale (after C. F. Richter). Magnitudes usually fall between 3 and 8 (notice, this scale is not written in Roman numerals). However, scientists can measure quakes so small they are felt only by very sensitive instruments. Some are so slight that negative numbers must be used to describe their size.

The 1906 San Francisco earthquake had a magnitude of 8.3. Larger earthquakes have been recorded at 8.8 and 8.9. This is the number you usually read about in newspapers when they describe the size of an earthquake. The story may read, "The magnitude of the earthquake was 4.6 on the Richter Scale." Newspapers often say that the scale runs from 0 to 10, but actually there is no bottom or top to the scale.

There is another thing that is usually not understood about this scale. An earthquake which has a magnitude of 8 is not twice as great as one that has a magnitude of 4. This is because the scale is *logarithmic*. This means that each number on the scale represents 10 times as much energy as the number below it. For instance, magnitude 8 is 10 times greater than magnitude 7. Magnitude 8 is 10 × 10 (or 100) times greater than magnitude 6. Magnitude 8 is 10 × 10 × 10 (or 1,000) times greater than magnitude 5. And it is a million times larger than magnitude 2 (10 × 10 × 10 × 10 × 10 × 10). So instead of magnitude 8 being twice as large as magnitude 4 (as some people mistakenly think), it is really 10,000 (10 × 10 × 10 × 10) times as great.

Will there be another disastrous earthquake in San Francisco? Small ones are frequently felt there, and one seismologist has said that, "The further you are from the last big earthquake, the nearer you are to the next."

Just as Caruso could not say why people keep building at the foot of Vesuvius, so we can-

This collapsed highway overpass is a result of an earthquake that shook California.

not explain the rebuilding of San Francisco. It is a beautiful location for a city. Built on seven hills, it sits on a peninsula that has the Pacific Ocean to the west and San Francisco Bay on the east. The sharpness of the hills and the blue of the Pacific endear the place to the people who live there.

In addition, man has a sort of blind faith that he can endure anything that nature can hand out. It is almost like a game to see if he can outwit natural disasters.

And so, whatever the reason, people all over the world continue to rebuild homes that have been destroyed by earthquakes.

CHAPTER FIVE

MESSINA,
ITALY
DECEMBER 28, 1908

SICILY, THE LARGEST ISLAND in the Mediterranean
Sea, is a triangular piece of land that lies just off
the toe of the Italian boot. It is only a little larger
than the state of New Hampshire and is separated
from the mainland by a narrow, treacherous strip
of water called the Strait of Messina.

It was in this strait that the legendary Greek
adventurer Ulysses met Scylla, the terrible sea
monster. Trying to steer his ship between the
island and the mainland, Ulysses was forced to
swing too close to the monster's cave to avoid a
huge whirlpool. Scylla, according to the legend,

captured and ate six of the Greek sailors from the ship.

From the time of Ulysses until the invention of safer ships, sailors always feared the Strait of Messina. The narrowness of the passage causes strong currents that can easily wash a ship onto the rocks.

But in spite of this, the town of Messina has been an important seaport since it was first settled by pirates in about 700 B.C. Standing very nearly at the northeastern tip of the island, the little city is only a few miles from Italy's mainland and a sister port there named Reggio. In 1908, Messina was Italy's eighth largest port, and was becoming an important vacation spot for tourists from the colder countries of Europe.

But Sicily is separated from the mainland by more than the Strait of Messina. Deep beneath the water in the strait lies a fault in the crust of the earth. Pressures that are constantly pushing up the mountains of Sicily and the Italian Peninsula are sometimes released by movements of the rocks along this huge crack. Within 15 years before 1908, three major earthquakes had damaged the houses and buildings that made up the town of Messina.

Early in the morning, about five o'clock, on December 28, 1908, these rocks slipped again. Actually there seems to have been two separate earthquakes just a few seconds apart. The first was not very violent and lasted for only a few seconds. The second quake shook the ground for perhaps eight seconds. Almost immediately a series of waves passed down the point of land upon which Messina stood. These shivers lasted for about 15 seconds. When they stopped, the cities of Messina and Reggio and dozens of villages for miles around lay in total ruin. Perhaps as many as 100,000 people were dead or dying.

Approximately half of the people in Messina were killed that morning in an earthquake that was barely felt on the other side of the island. There were several reasons for the size of this tragedy: the location of the town and the way its buildings were constructed; a large tsunami struck almost immediately; communications with the outside world were cut off by the earthquake; very cold, rainy weather; and, finally, the fact that no one in the area seemed able to take control of the rescue work.

A visitor to Messina in 1908 would have had to look very closely to discover that the town was not as solid and settled as it looked. It was a beautiful city, especially when seen for the first time from the deck of an approaching ship. Behind the busy quay and piers stood a row of lovely large buildings whose white walls shone in the sunlight. The harbor was well protected by a long, curving spit of sand, and its waters were dotted by brightly colored sailing boats. Once the visitor was on the docks he would be amazed to see the activity there, even in mid-winter. There were many large wooden barrels of oranges, limes, and lemons waiting to be loaded onto ships and taken to

northern ports. Here and there would be stacks
of marble slabs, also awaiting shipment. And in
the warehouses one might see bales of beautiful
silks that had been brought to Messina from
smaller ports on the mainland to be forwarded
from there to all parts of the world.

As he walked through the narrow streets, the
visitor would discover that much of the town was
built on level ground. But since there was not
much land between the harbor and the surrounding steep hills, most of the houses were
several stories tall. These, like the larger buildings
along the quay, were whitewashed and clean looking in the winter sun.

On three hills to the west of the city stood
ancient forts that reminded the visitor of the fact
that this city was more than 2,500 years old and
had been the battleground for several warring
countries over the centuries. Two of these forts
stood in abandoned ruin. The third now served
as a maximum security prison and contained 430
of Italy's most dangerous criminals, many of them
awaiting execution for their crimes.

Yes, this seemed to the visitor to be a very comfortable, safe little town. Since three tall, modern
hotels—the Trinacria, the France, and the Met-
ropole—stood near the center of the city it was no
wonder that hundreds of tourists flocked here
during the spring and autumn months. It was also
easy to understand why so many Englishmen and
their families had chosen this pretty place for their
retirement homes.

But wait. There is a cracked place in the wall
of that house. Looking closer, the visitor can see
that the houses are not as solid as they seem. In
spite of the fact that most are quite tall, their walls
are made of a mixture of river pebbles and bricks
held loosely together with sandy cement. Over this
unstable wall is spread plaster that has been
painted white.

And how about the streams that flow out of the
surrounding hills? There are five of them, all dry
in the winter. But it is easy to see that during the
rainy season they flow rapidly down the sides of
the steep hills, carrying a lot of loose soil and
rocks. When they hit the flat land around the harbor, they suddenly slow down and drop their
heavy load of soil. It doesn't take much looking
to discover that all of the flat land upon which the
center of the city is built is made up of this loose,
unstable, water-washed soil.

When the first shocks of the earthquake struck
this soft soil, the foundations of the houses tended
to shift. The unreinforced walls crumbled easily,
and the heavy tile roofs collapsed. Before the
ground settled down again, after perhaps less than
30 seconds of shaking, only three buildings
remained standing in all of Messina, and these
were badly damaged and later had to be
destroyed.

The earthquake was caused by a fault that lay
underwater, only a few miles offshore, somewhat
closer to the Italian mainland than to Sicily. And
it lay only a short distance underground. There-

fore, a tsunami smashed into the harbor at Messina. The wave was only seven feet high by the time it reached the harbor, but this was high enough. It swept across the sandspit, smashed the smaller boats in the harbor, and overwhelmed the quay and the piers. Many of the people who had managed to escape from the falling buildings had run to the dockside in the hope of finding a boat that would take them away from the fallen city. No one can even guess how many of these unfortunate people were standing on the quay when the wave washed over them.

A British seaman named Jabez Larkin was on board the *S.S. Drake* that night. The steamer had come to Messina to pick up the early fruit crops. Later Larkin wrote home about his experiences. He remembered being awakened by the shaking of the ship. He remembered everyone rushing up on the decks. Dust and the smell of sulfur filled the air, making it difficult to breathe. Choking and gasping, the young seaman felt his way along the deck through deep darkness. He could hear cries for help coming from the quay.

"Swing out the port lifeboats!" he heard the captain's voice from the direction of the bridge. "We must try to take those people on board."

Larkin and his fellow sailors quickly swung the lifeboats on the left side of the ship out over the water. But before they could lower them, the wave hit the side of the ship. It was lifted upward and then began to lean to its right. More and more the large ship leaned until Larkin was sure that it was going to turn over. But as the wave passed, the ship righted itself again. The men worked to unsnarl the lines to the boats, but they suddenly became aware that there were no more cries coming from the shore. Everyone, along with the stone quay, had been washed out to sea.

Across the Strait of Messina the tsunami damage was even worse. Several waves hit the unprotected shore and washed everything and everyone away. Some of these waves were nearly 40 feet high. In one place the wave picked up a block of cement weighing 20 tons and carried it 60 feet inland. Several large cement bridges on the mainland were smashed and thrown around by the tsunami.

Even in the best of times in 1908, Messina did not have very good communications with the outside world. A few poor roads wound up and over the hills that surrounded the town on the land side. There was one railroad line that skirted the seashore and ran around the island to the capital city of the state. And there was an undersea telegraph cable that connected the town with Reggio on the mainland. But all of these were smashed by the first shocks.

The telegraph cable was broken immediately. Even if it had not been, Reggio was badly hit itself. It is doubtful that anyone there would have been ready to take a message from the survivors in Messina. The railway was badly damaged, with rails broken and bridges down. Most of the men who knew how to run the trains were in the station that morning and 40 of them died when the roof of the building collapsed. The roads were cut in a dozen places by fissures and landslides and were impassable to anyone except a man on foot. It wasn't until well after dawn, several hours later, that a dazed, half-naked man stumbled into the nearest village to report the catastrophe.

One group of men managed to escape Messina by boat. They sailed across the strait, looking for safety and help in Reggio. But they found the city on the mainland in ruins, too. Together with a large group of people from Reggio and surrounding villages, they started walking up the coast. Two thousand people left Reggio. For ten hours they walked through the cold rain. Fifteen hundred of them dropped out along the way, many to die alongside the road. Late in the evening the 500 who were left staggered into Palmi, only to find this little town also without communications to the outside.

As it turned out, the damage at Messina was the first to be reported. The destruction of Reggio was not known to the rest of the world for nearly two days, and it was more than a week before every village in the area had been inspected.

Even the weather seemed to be against the people in the earthquake area. Usually the last part of December and the first few weeks of January could be counted on to be quite warm along the Strait of Messina. But in 1908–09, the winter was already bitter by Christmas. Since the earthquake struck in the early morning hours, most of the people were asleep. Few of them were lucky enough to be dressed warmly. Those trapped by the fallen buildings in exposed places froze to death before they could be rescued. Even those people who had managed to escape being trapped suffered terribly from the bitter cold.

But the biggest problem that faced the survivors of the earthquake was the fact that the leadership of the town had died in the falling buildings and no one from the outside seemed willing and able to take control. All of the officials of the city were either killed or were badly injured when their homes collapsed. The roof of the police barracks fell and killed 50 of the town's 57 policemen. The military barracks also collapsed and trapped all 800 of the soldiers who were asleep inside. Later, 14 of these men were dug out alive, but even then, until help was sent from Rome, Messina was without any official control. Furthermore, they were without medical help. The huge military hospital was destroyed, killing all of the patients and the medical staff. All but seven of the nuns in the convent died; these survivors acted as the only nurses the town had for several days.

On the hill to the west the prison walls fell. Most of the prisoners were killed in the collapse, but 30 dangerous men managed to escape. These men, mostly convicted murderers, prowled through the ruined city looking for loot and killing those people who tried to stop them.

Five people who had been guests of the large Trinacria Hotel were, along with hundreds of other people, rescued by the large ships that had

*This is what remained of a building in Messina, Sicily, in 1908
after the shocks of an earthquake traveled through the soft ground.*

managed to survive the tsunami in the harbor. A
hundred or more people were asleep in the
Trinacria that night, most of them foreigners visit-
ing Messina on business. On the top floor was a
London shipowner named Doresi. In the next
room was Charles Caiger, also English and a ship
architect. The third room, next to Caiger's, was
occupied by a Swedish family—a man, his wife,
and their small baby. All were awakened by the
shaking of the hotel and by the terrible noises of
the crashing buildings. They found themselves in
absolute darkness.

Caiger and Doresi called to each other and found that neither was hurt. They agreed that Doresi should try to find his way through the darkness to Caiger's room. He carefully felt his way along, not knowing that the outside wall of his room was completely gone.

Together in the dark, the men discussed what they should do. Then they heard a rapping on the wall. Calling out, they discovered that the Swedish family was also alive and wanted to join them. The five frightened people stayed together through the rest of the night in the total darkness, listening to the crashing of falling walls and the screams and calls for help that drifted up to them from the smashed hotel.

With the coming of the dawn they discovered that the three rooms in which they had slept were about all that was left of the hotel. The rest, right up to the walls of their rooms, had collapsed, killing more than 60 of the people who had been sleeping on the lower floors.

Dressing as warmly as they could, the five of them gathered up all the sheets and blankets they could find. They tied these into a long rope. The Swedish man tied his baby around his neck and climbed to the ground. His wife and the two Englishmen followed quickly. Together they made their way to the dock, climbing over piles of debris and dead bodies. At the ruined quayside they found the steamer *Afonwen*, a British ship out of Cardiff. Captain Owens, the ship's skipper, knew the Englishmen and took all five aboard and, later, took them to safety.

As soon as it was light enough to see, sailors from the *Afonwen* and from the *Drake*, which was tied up nearby, were sent ashore to do what they could for the people there. All through the day, small boats shuttled survivors from the shore to the ships. At ten o'clock that night the *S.S. Drake* sailed with more than 300 survivors aboard.

The Italian ships in the area were of little help. The government of that country seemed unable to recover from the disaster. The Italian battleship *Piemonte* was anchored in the harbor when the earthquake struck. Its commander, a Captain Passino, and most of his officers were ashore that night and were killed by the falling buildings. Those left on board refused to move without orders and so did nothing for 36 hours.

The Italian Navy's torpedo boat *Saffo* did land a small group of men. But this landing party stumbled upon the escaped prisoners who were busy trying to hack open the safe of the damaged Bank of Sicily, which contained a fortune of nearly $4,000,000. The robbers opened fire on the sailors and drove them back to their ship. The *Saffo* immediately set sail and left Messina's people to shift for themselves. Their excuse was that they had no orders.

Fortunately, the navies of other countries did not wait for orders. They didn't wait for an invitation from the Italian government either, since it was hopelessly snarled in red tape. At 11 o'clock on the morning of the earthquake a huge Russian battleship, the *Admiral Makiroff*, landed 600 men at the ruined quay. Many of these men were armed.

From the sea, as they approached the city, it seemed to the Russian seamen as if there had been little damage. The white buildings still stood along the waterfront, shining brightly in the sunlight. But as the men landed they realized that these were only the outer walls, forming hollow shells within which stood only rubble.

Two hours later, five British ships under the command of Admiral Sir H. G. Curzon-Howe arrived and put more men ashore. For the next week, the weight of the rescue operations rested on the shoulders of these uninvited guests.

The Russian sailors soon discovered the attempted bank robbery. Instead of running, they returned the robbers' gunfire and killed several. The rest escaped, leaving the safe unbroken. Russian sailors stood guard over the bank until Italian soldiers and bank officials finally arrived.

An open-air hospital was established on the docks and both the Russian sailors and those from the British ships began searching for injured people. Soon a heavy, cold rain began to fall and the hospital was moved into a shattered building. Somehow, in spite of the rain, this building caught fire and 100 of the patients there burned to death.

There were many tales of heroic rescues by these men. A friendly competition soon was working, each navy trying to rescue more people than the other. Two Russian sailors managed to rescue a total of 110 injured people during the eight days they worked. Another Russian team used ropes to scale the tottering wall of a demolished building, even though the entire tower of plaster and pebbles shook with the tremors that still ran through the ground. From 30 feet above the ground, they managed to save an injured woman who had clung there for nearly 12 hours.

A group of British sailors were attracted by a voice coming from a pile of rubble. "Maria!" Someone was calling from below. "Maria! Maria!" Carefully the sailors began to dig through the smashed plaster, roofing tiles, and broken walls. They soon broke through into a cellar. One man was lowered into the dark hole where the sound of the name being called came constantly.

Once in the dark underground room, the sailor struck a match. With each shiver of the ground, plaster dust filtered through the air and the pile of rubble above his head groaned. The room seemed empty. But the cry came again. "Maria! Maria!" Following the sound, the sailor looked behind a pile of fallen wood and saw the source of the cries—a large, green parrot!

The sailor laughed, picked up the bird, and started back out of the hole. But then he stopped. Perhaps, he thought, the bird was actually calling to someone. Handing the parrot out, the sailor went back down into the buried room to make one more search. This time he found a closed door. Forcing it open, he discovered another room. On

the floor lay the unconscious body of a young girl.
Both she and her parrot recovered.

Kitchens on board the ships were kept busy preparing hot food for the survivors. The British
officers and their men refused to eat anything
other than the cold emergency rations, saving the
hot food for the earthquake's victims. Shipping
companies of many countries ordered their ships
to divert from their routes and take what food,
blankets, clothing, and medical supplies they could
spare to Messina. After stripping their ships of all
extra supplies, these ships loaded as many people
as possible on board and took them to the mainland.

Where was the U.S. Navy? Just a few hours
away, in the Red Sea. Unlike the British and Russian commanders, the American admiral waited
for a call for help from the Italian king. But the
invitation never came.

The reason for this strange behavior was, to the
admiral at least, a good one. Just two years before,
in January of 1907, an earthquake had struck the
island of Jamaica. Three ships from the U. S.
Navy landed almost immediately to help. The gov-
ernor of the island at the time was very anti-
American and had accused the United States of
"invading" his island "with armed troops." Not
wanting to be criticized again, the U. S. Navy
waited and was finally criticized by most of the
world for *not* helping!

Four days after the earthquake, on New Year's
Day, the Italian government finally ordered sol-

diers into Messina. More than 11,000 troops
landed that day, but they found that they had to
spend their time trying to prevent looting and
restoring law and order. The damaged area had
become flooded with people from the outside,
some looking for lost relatives and others looking
for something to steal. The troops divided the city
into four sectors. They patrolled the area and shot
looters on sight. During the next day, 50 people
were shot and killed while looting the ruined
stores or stealing from the pockets of the dead.

Food rationing was begun, but there was still not
enough food to feed the thousands of people in
the city. Dogs and cats were caught, killed, and
eaten by the hungry survivors.

On January fifth, the Italian general who was
in charge of the town decided that the danger of
disease spreading from the rotting corpses to the
living people was becoming too great. He ordered
the foreign sailors to leave the port and had his
soldiers surround the ruins. Every person who
could not prove that he had good reason to stay
was taken aboard a ship and moved to another
port.

It was only now that the Italians could turn their
attention to the small villages inland from Messina
and along the coast of the strait. The isolated ham-
lets, damaged as badly as the larger cities of Messina and Reggio, had been without food or medical supplies for more than a week. Hundreds of
people died in these villages, many because help
had not arrived in time.

On the next day, January sixth, the archbishop of Messina climbed to the top of a ruined wall and blessed the people whose bodies lay in the rubble. Then quicklime was scattered over the debris and mass burials began. Short, violent shocks were still running through the ground and occasionally a wall would crumble, crushing a rescuer or a trapped person below.

The general knew that many people still lived in the destroyed town, trapped by the debris but not yet dead. On January fifth, another 37 people had been rescued alive. But he knew that he had to act. The threat of disease and the danger from the still-standing walls were too great. So he ordered the quicklime to be spread and the standing walls to be dynamited.

The crews of workmen and government officials, who searched through the ruins for buried art treasures and money, continued to find living people and to save them before they died in the leveling of the town. On the sixth, a total of ten people were found. On the eighth, nine more were taken out alive.

On the ninth, an Italian soldier arrived at one of the army posts. He was on leave from his unit and was supposed to have arrived in Messina on the 31st, to spend the New Year's holiday with his fiancee. During the night of the eighth he dreamed that the girl was alive and was calling to him from the ruins of her home. So he quickly got a ride across the strait on a small boat. Only half convinced, the officer in charge allowed the young man to lead a small group of soldiers to the place where the girl's house had stood. Digging through the ruins they found the girl, only slightly injured, in the basement of the shattered house.

As the dynamite explosions rocked the ruined town, more people were taken out safely. On January 12, more than two weeks after the quake, a three-year-old child was found lying under the bodies of his parents. On the 15th, two girls and their baby brother were found in a cellar where they had lived for 18 days on raw vegetables and olive oil. Later that same day a five-year-old boy and a 70-year-old woman, alive but unable to speak, were taken from the ruins.

These were the last to be saved. On the 16th, another earthquake tremor shook the town and leveled the ruins. More dynamiting was not needed. In the cold rain, the last of the survivors abandoned Messina for what they assumed would be forever.

But offers of help to rebuild the city came in from many countries all over the world. The United States shipped in 3,000 pre-fabricated houses along with carpenters who were to teach the Italians how to put them up. Swiss and German money flowed in to help build orphanages. And so Messina began to live again.

At first it was planned that the new city would be built to the south of the old site. But the nearly perfect natural harbor was too valuable to abandon. So, in 1912, work began on rebuilding Messina on its original site.

This time the city was built with a plan. The ruins of the former buildings were leveled and cement was poured into them to make a solid base. Strict building codes were established and every building in the town followed them. Heights were limited to two stories at first, and reinforced concrete walls were insisted upon. Later, as the city grew, buildings up to four stories were allowed. Streets were planned so as to be wide enough not to be blocked if the buildings on both sides fell.

Messina is now perhaps the only city in the world to be entirely "earthquake-proof." No major earthquake has occurred in the area since the city was rebuilt, but the British invasion of Sicily in 1943, during World War II, proved to the world that the city could withstand the worst earthquake. During the invasion, 4,000 tons of high explosives rained down on the town. Later, the British soldiers found very little shock damage to the buildings that had not received direct hits.

CHAPTER SIX

THE KWANTO EARTHQUAKE SEPTEMBER 1, 1923

THE FIRST DAY OF SEPTEMBER in the year 1923 dawned bright and clear over the coastal plain that lies to the north of Sagami Bay. A soft breeze blew steadily from the south and, as the noon hour approached, the temperature began to climb.

A large house stood on a small hill overlooking the bay and the narrow beach of sand that marked its edge. The rear parts of the house were typically Japanese in design, but someone had added a few Western-style rooms and a broad, shaded porch to the front. Because of this, the house had been rented almost constantly by foreigners for many years.

Two of its present occupants sat on the big porch. The boy, a twelve-year-old American, was reading. The man had come to Japan from Denmark many years before as a reporter, but now he spent his time painting and sketching.

"How is the book, Shrimp?" the man asked, as he bent to add a drop of watercolor to the paper spread on the table before him.

The boy looked up and smiled at the funny nickname that was the only name anyone used for him. He liked the men that his father worked with. Most of them were writers, like his father. Or, like the big Dane, had once been writers.

"It's a great book," he answered. "When is my father coming home? Do you know?"

"He will be home this weekend, I am certain. Perhaps he is on the way now. He just went up to Tokyo to check on the new minister whom the emperor has appointed. He will probably take the electric train down to Yokohama and check at the docks to see if anything from America has arrived for you. Then he will get hold of a car somewhere and drive home."

"Do you think we will have something from home?" the boy asked with excitement in his voice.

"I doubt it. That storm we had two days ago was a pretty bad one. A typhoon like that would cause all of the ships in this part of the Pacific to change course for quite a while. Perhaps your boxes will be in next week."

"The Shrimp" stood up, carefully marked his place in the book, and stretched. He looked at the beach, crowded with swimmers and sunbathers.

"I think I'll go for a swim before lunch," he said.

At that moment, thirty-five miles to the north, the boy's father made his way through the crowds that always seemed to be on the sidewalks of Tokyo. As clock hands moved closer to 12, thousands of people left their desks and searched for places to eat lunch. Some hurried toward restaurants that soon would be filled. Others searched for cool, grassy spots in the city's many parks. Others, like Henry Kenney, had business that kept them from eating exactly at noon.

Kenney had hoped to be on his way home before this. After the week-long rainstorm, it seemed that everyone in Tokyo who could get away for the weekend was planning to do so. "The train will be crowded," he thought to himself as he pushed his way toward the station. "And so will the docks in Yokohama."

He liked Yokohama better than Tokyo, as most foreigners did, even though he had to ride the bumping, jolting little electric train up to the capital city several times a week. Tokyo, with 2½ million people, was the sixth largest city in the world, and much too large for his liking. It had grown from an ancient settlement that flanked each bank of the Sumida River, and sometimes travel across the river was nearly impossible as the bridges became clogged with people. Away from the river in both directions stretched narrow and twisting streets, always clogged with people, carts, and cars.

Yokohama, on the other hand, was much smaller—perhaps with only one-fifth as many people. It was surrounded by high hills that pushed it against a large harbor. Many Western-style buildings had been built in the business district that had naturally grown up around the edges of the shipping area. It was here that he and the writers he knew preferred to work.

Both cities perched on the western banks of Tokyo Bay. Kenney, his son, and the Danish painter preferred to live about 15 miles south of Yokohama, near the resort town of Kamakura on the beach at the northeastern end of Sagami Bay. It was a good place for a boy to grow up, Kenney thought, as he shoved his way into the little railway car.

Someone was waving to him from across the car. The man was an old friend, an English reporter traveling to Yokohama. Kenney greeted him as he fit into the tiny seat across the aisle. The train started smoothly and picked up speed as it left the station.

In a building not far away, a world-famous scientist, Professor Akitsume Imamura, was also going to skip his lunch. Imamura was a seismologist, a geologist who specializes in the study of earthquakes. At about the time that Kenney's train was leaving the station, the seismograph machines at Tokyo Imperial University's laboratory began to move. Imamura and his staff stood around the machines, watching the needles move back and forth.

Japan has been called "The World's Earthquake Factory" and so it was natural that Imamura's laboratory should be the best in the world. Japanese scientists and builders have studied earthquakes for perhaps more years than have any other group of people. Since long before the Lisbon earthquake, the builders of that country have tried to find ways to make buildings more resistant to earthquake damage.

Imamura himself had long been convinced that the larger cities of his country were poorly planned to withstand a major earthquake shock. Twenty years earlier he had warned that the streets of Tokyo were too narrow and that the water mains were too likely to be broken.

"One hundred thousand people could die," he warned. "We need wider streets, protected supplies of water to fight fires with, and more open spaces in which people could gather to escape falling debris."

But Tokyo was too big to be rebuilt. Much of it stood on low land that had been deposited by the frequent floods of the Sumida River. Many of its older houses were made of bamboo and paper, and had heavy tile roofs. These building materials were not only cheap but they were available almost everywhere and were easy to use. Besides, some people said, a major shock had not hit Tokyo for many, many years.

Even Imamura did not believe that the shaking of the seismograph machines that he watched at noon on September 1, 1923, showed the beginning of a major earthquake. He had lived through hundreds of quakes, some of them rather large, and he felt that he knew how the large ones started. He watched the timers on the machines and during the 12th second of shaking a large jolt ran through the building.

"That should be the major shock," he told one of his fellow scientists. "They should begin to become less strong now."

But the shaking of the building continued and the seismograph machines swung wider and wider. The crashing of tiles falling from the roof could be heard through the laboratory's thick walls. Then the entire building began to rock like a boat in a high wind.

Kenney's son was standing on the porch of their house in Kamakura, looking at the inviting water below them. Without any warning of any kind, the roof of the porch collapsed. Splintered wooden beams and broken tiles buried both people before they knew what was happening to them. One huge beam smashed across the back of the painter, while another threw the boy to the floor, pinning him by the legs.

"Shrimp!" the man called from the pile of debris. "Can you get out, Shrimp? Get away from the house. I can't make it," he said, and then he died.

The boy struggled to free himself, but his legs were tightly held by the fallen roof. The ground shook harder and harder, and a growling seemed to come from the ground beneath the shattered house. Then a louder roar drowned out all other noises. He looked toward the beach and saw a wall of water rushing down on the people who, moments before, had been enjoying the sun and water. The 16-foot-high wave swept across the narrow stretch of sand, overwhelmed the people there, smashed the seawall into pebbles, and crossed the garden toward the house. As the water lapped at the foundations of the house, the Japanese servants who had worked for the Americans for many years pulled "The Shrimp" from the wreckage and to safety.

Kenney's train had just passed Omori, a suburb of Tokyo, when the car began to pitch up and down. Then it began to sway from side to side. The passengers clung to their seats to keep from being thrown into the aisles.

"*Jishin!*" (Earthquake!) The word passed from person to person through the train.

Kenney looked through the window of the rocking car. The stone face of an embankment suddenly broke loose and shot down the slope as they passed. A four-story building vanished in a cloud of cement dust. Roofing tiles smashed onto the ground alongside the train.

The train slowed and then stopped its forward motion but continued to buck and rock as it stood on the tracks. The conductor made his way through the excited passengers to the front of the car. Removing his cap he said politely and calmly, "I am sorry. This train will not proceed further toward Yokohama."

Kenney and his English friend got quickly down from the train. The right-of-way along the tracks was crowded with people from the nearby town who were trying to find open ground away from the falling buildings.

"No wonder the train had to stop!" The Englishman pointed up the tracks.

The pair looked with amazement as the rails writhed and wiggled like snakes ahead of the train. More tiles were thrown from the roofs around them. Large cracks began to appear in the walls of nearby houses. Realizing that the roads would soon be impassable to anyone except a man on foot, the two men decided to try to walk out of the damaged area. Neither realized that they were not in the center of the earthquake and that they would have to walk the entire 35 miles to Kamakura.

"We had better hurry," the Englishman said. "Looks like another storm blowing up." Ahead of them a huge cloud appeared on the horizon, growing swiftly. It was thick and black against the bright blue of the sky. The south wind blew it quickly toward the two men as they began their long walk toward the town of Kamakura.

They followed the railroad tracks, expecting to cross the Tamagawa River on the bridge that had been built for the railroad. But when they reached the river they found the bridge twisted and smashed. The supporting piers had been rocked out of place and the rails hung in the air, almost without support. Amazingly, however, a small footbridge made of only two boards laid side-by-side was undamaged. Carefully they made their way across the river on this, always thinking,

"What would happen if another shock caught us here?"

At the end of the bridge they found the river bank had sunk and split and they had to jump to it. On their right was a pile of bricks and wood that they recognized as the remains of a sugar mill. Fire licked up through the debris. The wind, now blowing strongly from the west, fanned the flames until the iron machines within the damaged building began to melt from the heat.

Farther on was a large electric plant, one wall caved in like a shoe box that had been kicked. They saw no one anywhere. Were all of the workers in the two buildings trapped in the rubble?

"I had hoped that we would be out of the damaged area once we crossed the river," Kenney told his friend. "But it seems to be just as bad here."

"Let's see how Kawasaki looks," the Englishman suggested.

Kawasaki was a large village that stood a short distance ahead. Most of the houses in the town were made of wood and many of them had been two stories. All of those that the two men first passed were completely destroyed. The wooden boards looked as if they had been torn, like paper, by some gigantic hand. Jumbles of shattered wood and tiles blocked the streets, and the travelers had to climb over these mounds as they moved through the town.

On the south end of the village, however, there seemed to be less damage. They began to pass houses that were only partly damaged. Then they found a pottery dealer's shop whose delicate merchandise had escaped undamaged. Brightly decorated dishes, teapots, rice bowls, and saki cups stood safe under a roof that only half covered them. They rattled gently with the shivers that still ran almost steadily through the earth.

Across the road stood another nearly undamaged shop. A sign across its front announced that cold beer could be bought inside. The two weary men looked at each other.

"It looks like we are getting out of the worst of it," the Englishman said.

"Yes," Kenney agreed. "We should be able to get a ride shortly. Let's take time for a beer, if they have any left."

"Sounds good. I have never been this dry since I came to Japan. It's usually humid, especially just before a rain." He waved toward the black cloud that still stood on the horizon to the south. "But today it's as hot and dry as the desert."

"Perhaps the rain will miss us. The wind has changed and is blowing the cloud away from us."

The inside of the shop was a jumble of overturned furniture and pottery. "Yes," they were told, "we have beer. But it is not very cold." They laughed at having to help the shopkeeper hunt through the rubble for an opener and they felt certain that the worst was over.

But as they sipped at their drinks, two young Japanese men came into the shop, asking for something to drink. Their clothing was dirty and torn.

"What news do you have from the south?"
someone asked them.

"Yokohama is gone!" they told the shopkeeper.
"All of the waterfront collapsed, and now she is
burning."

They pointed toward the towering cloud that
Kenney and his friend had thought was an
approaching rainstorm. "That is the smoke from
the oil tanks. The whole city is on fire."

The two men were almost running as they
moved down the road toward the burning city.
Occasionally they passed houses that were on fire,
apparently set by cooking fires that had been
upset by the earthquake. The ground still shook
under them from time to time and they were constantly afraid that one of them might prove to be
another major shock.

They found the village of Higashikanagawa
almost entirely in flames. Their path blocked, they
returned to the railroad right-of-way. There they
found many people from the village, squatting
quietly, watching their homes burn.

Leaving the railroad tracks, the men returned
to the road. They passed many isolated fires and
the damage seemed to be even more complete
here than it had been farther north. They reached
the hills that surrounded Yokohama on the land
side and started up the steep road toward the
crest.

"Listen!" Kenney called, stopping his friend
with a touch on the arm. "What's that noise?"

The men stopped and listened.

"It sounds like the sea. Like waves smashing against the shore."

"But we are miles from the ocean."

"It's fire! It's the roar of flames!"

They ran up the slope, passing people going the opposite direction carrying furniture and bundles of belongings. At the top of the ridge they stopped in horror. Below them, within the half-bowl of the hills, was a sea of fire. Here and there, a broken wall stood like an island. It seemed as if there was nothing of Yokohama left to burn and that the earth itself was on fire.

As they stared hopelessly at the ruins below, other people joined them. Each had a terrible story to tell of the horror they had lived through.

The first shock was "like a bucking horse" someone said. "In the space of time it would take to clap your hands three times the city was gone."

The people who survived the falling of the buildings rushed into the streets, which were blanketed by a fog of dust. This was blown away by the wind, which had suddenly changed directions and blew briskly from the west. Some thought only of escape and scrambled over the piles of debris that completely blocked every street. Others clawed in the rubble for friends and family who were trapped there.

Almost immediately, the fires began. All of the city's fire fighting equipment had been destroyed by the falling buildings. Even if it had not been, the firemen would have been unable to get through the streets because of the piles of cement,

wood, and bricks that blocked them all. The water
mains had broken in hundreds of places and
would have made the use of fire hydrants impossible.

Unchecked, the fires spread quickly, fanned by
the wind that had now reached nearly gale force.
Small fires soon joined with other individual fires
until entire city blocks burned. The wind from the
west forced the fire steadily toward the waterfront.
People trapped in the collapsed buildings had to
be left behind to burn to death as the heat drove
the rescuers away.

As more and more buildings caught fire, people
were forced into the few open squares and parks
in the center of town. A few lucky people found
the broken mains had flooded one square to a
depth of about a foot. They sat down in the water
and ducked under when the heat became too
great. Hair and clothing would suddenly burst
into flame and nearby people would slap wet mud
on the person to put out the fire.

Other people were not so fortunate. Those who
looked for safety in small ponds were killed as the
temperature of the water increased nearly to the
boiling point.

The harbor itself was soon burning. Oil tanks
were burst by the quake and the oil dumped into
the water. This soon caught fire and carried the
flames throughout the dock area. At the dock a
Canadian Pacific mail steamer was preparing to
leave for Vancouver. With steam already up, it
managed to cast off and get safely away from the

burning buildings. Until about 5 p.m., when the wind died, the ship was busy dodging burning ships, burning patches of oil, and floating debris. As the 50 mile-an-hour wind died, small boats were sent back to the dock to pick up survivors. Hundreds of people were able to escape the burning city in this way.

These stories made Kenney even more afraid for the safety of his son. Leaving the group of people on the hilltop, he and his English friend walked inland around the burning city. The wind, which had shifted first to the west and then to the north, had prevented the fire from reaching the northwestern corner of the city. Here, as night fell, the two foreigners walked through an area of mud-and-thatch houses. These buildings appeared to have been squashed flat, much as if they had been stepped on by a giant foot.

A man with a small lantern passed by, leading a group of people south, out of the city. The Westerners were invited to join the group. By the light of the lantern they felt their way through the darkness. Fissures in the earth had to be crossed. Blocks of land between the fissures were often tilted at weird angles. Progress was slow, but finally the little group reached the village of Ofuna, only two miles from Kamakura. There they stopped to rest at the undamaged railroad station.

Kenney asked the station master for word of the resort town. "Kamakura was smashed flat and is burning," he was told. "There is nothing left."

This frightening news washed the fatigue from the American and he struck out through the darkness alone. A sliver of a moon and burning farmhouses lit his way through the darkness. Soon he found himself on the road leading to the beach. Large trees had been thrown in every direction and lay like pick-up-sticks across the road. As he climbed through their branches and over their trunks he thought about how to cross the large river that flowed between him and his home. He guessed that the bridge would have been destroyed by the earthquake. So he decided to follow the beach and swim across the mouth of the river.

But when he arrived at the river, he found it nearly dry. Its bottom and much of the bottom of the bay had been raised nearly six feet by the earthquake. He was able to cross the wide river, barely getting his feet wet.

He searched his empty house which, though badly damaged, still stood. Then he heard the faint sound of sticks being struck together and the drone of voices. In the rear of the ruined house he found his servants, holding a Buddhist ceremony of thanksgiving. Here he finally learned that "The Shrimp" was safe, taken to the hills by Japanese neighbors.

It was many days before help arrived. On Tuesday, three days after the disaster, a Japanese Navy destroyer arrived offshore from Kamakura. But the ship was there to take away the body of a Japanese princess who had been killed in the town, and not to help the survivors. On Thursday a flock of American destroyers arrived, and three hours later they were joined by British ships. These landed tons of supplies for the survivors and took aboard those people who wanted to go to Tokyo.

Kenney was one of those taken to Tokyo. There he found a disaster nearly as large as that in Yokohama. Only six large buildings, each made of reinforced concrete, remained standing. The shocks of the earthquake did little damage except among the Japanese-style houses that had been built on the unsolid land along the river. But in Tokyo the fires had been worse than those in Yokohama. Within 48 hours, 400,000 buildings in a seven-square-mile area were burned to ashes. Much of the University was burned, although Professor Imamura's valuable records were saved. Art collections, libraries, historical records whose value could not be estimated were all lost. And with them, thousands and thousands of people.

As in Yokohama, the people of Tokyo hurried to open spaces to avoid the falling buildings and the fires. Along the eastern bank of the river stood a 250-acre open area next to the military clothing depot. By mid-afternoon, 45,000 people were crowded into this park. The clothing depot caught fire at about 4 p.m. and the buildings on the other three sides of the square also began to burn quickly. Fanned by a 50-mile-an-hour wind, the flames reached tremendous temperatures. Billows of smoke poured into the open field. Small tornadoes, caused by the updraft above the fires, picked up people and flung them around like paper dolls. Only those who managed to reach the water of the river survived. The rest died of burns or were suffocated by the smoke.

The final toll from the earthquake-fire-tsunami was terrible. In Yokohama, 27,000 lay dead, more than 40,000 were injured, and 65 percent of the buildings in the city was destroyed. In Tokyo, 100,000 bodies lay in the ruins of half the city, and another 40,000 were injured seriously. Elsewhere in the Kwanto Plain, two million houses were destroyed and another 12,000 people were added to the list of dead.

This national catastrophe seriously affected an area of land roughly 90 miles by 60 miles, or more than 5,000 square miles. Yet the shocks were felt over only about 160,000 square miles, as compared with the million square miles of both the Lisbon and the New Madrid quakes. Aside from the tremendous loss of life, this earthquake produced some very unusual results:

—The bottom of Sagami Bay apparently sank as much as 600 feet near its center, where the epicenter of the earthquake was located. At the same time, land at the north end of the bay was raised as much as 750 feet. Changes in the level of land features during earthquakes are not unusual, but no one can explain why these changes should have been so large.

—Tile pipes which used to line the walls of deep wells in one part of the Kwanto Plain were shaken out of the ground until they stood ten feet above the surface, like narrow, tile chimneys.

—In one district, potatoes growing in the fields were reported to have been thrown from the ground by the passing shock waves.

—A mudflow 200 yards wide and 50 feet deep picked up an entire train and carried it into the bay, killing more than 200 people.

—The pilings of an ancient bridge, buried for 700 years, were shaken to the surface by the earthquake. They were found standing upright in solid earth, like ghosts of the forgotten past.

—The aftershocks continued for more than two years, until most people became so used to them that they didn't notice when the ground shivered. During the month of September, 1923, Professor Imamura's seismographs recorded 1,256 shocks. These continued until, in November of 1925, Professor Imamura announced that the earthquake was officially over and that everything was normal—with only two shocks a day!

Japan rebuilt its cities, of course. Aid poured in from all over the world and the mistakes of the past were not repeated. The rebuilding of Tokyo and Yokohama was carefully planned. The plans included constructing stronger buildings that could withstand the earthquake shocks, wider streets that could not be blocked by falling buildings, and water mains that would not be broken easily by the moving earth. Also included were many parks and open spaces where people could go to avoid both falling buildings and raging fires.

CHAPTER SEVEN

HEBGEN LAKE, MONTANA AUGUST 17, 1959

THE WESTERN ONE-THIRD of the state of Montana has been crumpled by pressures within the earth into high mountains of tremendous beauty. Evergreen forests of pine, spruce, and fir coat the sides of the steep slopes that often reach more than 11,000 feet above sea level. Broad valleys have been cut through the mountains by dozens of rivers.

Along the top of the mountains runs the Continental Divide. Water that falls on the slopes to the west of this imaginary line eventually finds its way to the Pacific Ocean. Rain or melted snow that flows down the eastern slopes passes through a series of rivers until it finally reaches the Gulf of Mexico.

One of the major rivers on the eastern side of the Continental Divide in Montana is the Madison River. The river actually begins in Yellowstone Park, which lies in the northwestern corner of Wyoming.

It has cut a narrow gorge only a few miles west of the border of Yellowstone Park and near the point where Montana, Wyoming, and Idaho meet. During the summer months thousands of tourists enjoy camping along the river, looking at the natural beauty of the area, and learning the exciting history of its people. During the weekend of August 15 and 16, 1959, more than 350 people were crowded along the river in the gorge. Many of these campers had spent their vacation in the park itself. Others had roamed the mountains, returning to the peaceful river bank at night. Some had fished in the cold waters of Hebgen Lake or had caught trout in the Madison River.

Hebgen Lake was created in 1915 by an 87-foot-high dam built by the Montana Power Company. The dam blocked the Madison River gorge and backed up a long, narrow, winding lake that soon became lined with fishing camps, summer homes, and small dude ranches. Below the dam, in the narrow, eight-mile-long canyon, hundreds of campsites and cabins were built between the river bank and Highway 287. Across the river, to the south, stands a steep ridge, the top of which is nearly 7,600 feet above sea level. It was in this beautiful canyon below Hebgen Dam that many summer visitors liked to pitch their tents and park their trailers.

On Sunday night many of the people left the valley; so by Monday night, August 17, fewer than 200 people were camped along the river. Most of these were in or near Rock Creek campground at the opposite end of the gorge from Hebgen Dam. The others were in two other campsites in the gorge itself and in scattered camps along the eight-mile stretch of river.

Perhaps some of these people knew that earthquakes occasionally shook this part of the United States. The Madison range of mountains, that runs to the north in a long, narrow string from Hebgen Lake, began to form about 50 million years ago. Tremendous pressures from within the earth slowly pushed against the rocks lying under an ancient, shallow sea until, folded and wrinkled, cracked and broken, they were pushed upward. This birth of a mountain range was not a quick one. The uplifting of these peaks to over 11,000 feet above the sea's surface was a slow process. Indeed, the pressures continue to push the rocks upward today. Sometimes these pressures become too great for the strength of the rocks. When they do, the rocks break and slip, and earthquake shocks hit the area.

But it had been many, many years since an earthquake had done any serious damage in Montana. Few of the people in the Madison River canyon in 1959 remembered the quake of 1925. And those who did remember probably did not know that had it occurred 60 seconds earlier it would have buried a transcontinental train and its passengers under a huge landslide. Perhaps a few more of the campers remembered the full week of earthquakes that had shaken Helena, Montana, hundreds of times during October, 1935, and had damaged 80 percent of the capital city's property. It is almost certain that none of the vacationers was thinking of the possibility of earthquakes at 22 minutes before midnight on August 17, 1959.

In a small travel trailer a short distance upstream from the Rock Creek campground, Polly Weston was baking bread. Her husband, Hal, had just put the coffeepot on the stove and the couple was chatting as they waited for the coffee to heat. Outside, Stephen and Bill Conley, teen-age nephews of the Westons, were asleep in the car.

Bears had been prowling the campsite all through the weekend. The night before, a man from a neighboring campsite had frightened a bear away by throwing a can of fruit at it. And, only a few hours before, the Weston's dog Peanuts had chased a bear up a nearby tree. So when the trailer suddenly began to shake, it was perhaps natural that the Weston's first thoughts were that the bears had returned. But Peanuts slept quietly.

"Some watchdog!" Mrs. Weston said as she reached for the coffeepot. But before she touched it, the pot slid quickly across the top of the stove and onto the floor of the trailer.

Mr. Anthony Schreiver, from Billings, Montana, also thought of bears when he felt the first shock of the earthquake. He, his wife, and their seven-year-old daughter Bonnie were asleep in their trailer only a few yards away from the Westons. All three were awakened by the violent heaving of their trailer.

"There's that bear again!" Mr. Schreiver said to his wife. Fearing that the animal would frighten his mother-in-law who was asleep in a second trailer a few feet away, he got sleepily out of bed. "I'll scare it away," he said. Grabbing a flashlight, he started toward the door.

Asleep in a tent in the next campsite were Mr. and Mrs. Warren Steele. Mr. Steele worked in a meat packing plant in Billings and was a friend of the Schreivers. He awoke to feel the tent twisting back and forth, as if a strong wind were blowing against it. Knowing that he had not tied the tent down very tightly, Mr. Steele got out of his sleeping bag and went out into the night. To his surprise he found the moon shining brightly and the air calm and clear.

For some reason that no one understands, Mrs. Mildred Greene felt a much more violent shock than did the Steeles. Ray and Mildred Greene and their nine-year-old son Steve had just finished a short vacation in Glacier National Park near the Canadian border. They had spent most of the day driving south, toward their home in Billings. The quiet Madison River canyon had long been a favorite camping spot of theirs. So, as they often did, they detoured out of their way in order to spend one night in the pleasant Rock Creek camp. All three were asleep in their tent next to the tumbling river, upstream from their neighbors from Billings. The first shock threw them all violently around. Mrs. Greene scrambled to her feet only to be thrown roughly to the ground again. Mr. Greene called to his son and all three rushed out into the moonlight.

An elderly couple in a nearby trailer was also thrown around by the first shock of the earthquake. Grover and Lillian Mault, both near 70, had just gone to bed when they felt the trailer move as if it were rolling down a hill. They stumbled out of bed and were knocked to the floor.

Not everyone in the campground felt the earthquake tremor. The Purley R. Bennett family was so tired that they apparently slept through the shaking. They had spent the day touring Virginia City, Montana's reconstructed 1865 gold camp. They had planned to spend the night camping in the Madison River gorge and then to follow Highway 287 into Yellowstone National Park early the next day.

They had arrived at the campground late and everyone complained of being tired. Rather than put up the tent, Mr. Bennett and his wife Irene had gone to sleep in their station wagon. In sleeping bags on the ground nearby were 16-year-old Phillip and his two brothers and sister. A roaring sound woke the parents. As they lay there, listening, a second roar that was even louder than the first crashed through the trees. Deciding that they had better check on the children, both parents left the car and walked through the shadows toward the huddled figures.

Phillip, too, had been wakened by the roaring noise. He looked up from his sleeping bag in disbelief as he saw the top of the mountain ridge across the river break loose and cascade down toward him. A tremendous wind that pushed ahead of the mass of rock that was now moving at about 100 miles-an-hour lifted him into the air. As he flew through the air, the heavy sleeping bag was torn from him and so was most of his clothing. The wind carried him along for a while and then threw him violently into wildly swirling water. Helpless, he was carried along, smashing into rocks and trees until he lost consciousness.

Meanwhile, his mother did not see the mountainside collapse but she felt the blast of the wind. The wind grew stronger until she was blown to the ground, sheltered a little by a large tree. Helplessly she watched her husband struggle against the force of the wind. He grabbed a small tree for support and then, as his feet lifted from the ground, he lost his grip and disappeared into the darkness. A bundle she feared might be her daughter tumbled past in the hurricane-strength wind, and a car rolled over and over past her.

Hal Weston saw the mountain fall also. As Polly knelt on the floor of their trailer to mop up the spilled coffee, Hal glanced out the window.

"The mountain! It's moving!" he shouted.

Through the window, the Westons could see trees sailing through the air toward them. Then branches, rocks, and finally tree trunks began smashing into the now rocking trailer. The Westons rushed outside, quickly collected the startled boys from the car, and ran up the slope, pushed by the growing wind. As they ran, they heard the screams of the injured and frightened campers all around them.

Warren Steele, surprised to find the night so still, stood by his tent looking for the cause of the shaking his camp had received. He looked up into the clear sky and, finding no clouds there, glanced at the ridge across the river from the camp. In the bright moonlight it looked to him as if the mountain were on fire, with huge billows of smoke rising from it. Then, as he watched, the whole face of the ridge began to move. He realized then that it was clouds of dust, not smoke, that he had seen.

The wall of rocks and dirt hit the river with the speed of an express train and forced the water out of the bank ahead of it. Water began running through Steele's tent. As he called to his wife, Mr. Steele realized the water was becoming rapidly deeper and he could feel a strong current. Together, the Steeles struggled through the rising water. As they fought through the darkness, Mr. Steele lost his footing and was washed away by the black, swirling water.

As the frightened Greene family left their tent, they looked toward the river. A waist-high wall of water rushed toward them. Trees, some with roots

still attached to them, tumbled around in the tor-
rent. Rocks rolled along, pushed by the advancing
flood. As the wave hit them, Steve disappeared and
then bobbed to the surface again. His father caught
him before he could be carried off and the three of
them struggled toward their station wagon.

The car's engine started without difficulty, but
the car would not move. Later the Greenes discovered that several large pine trees had been wedged
under the wheels of the car. In the beam of their
headlights, the Greenes watched helplessly as the
flood washed around them.

Ray Painter and his wife, of Ogden, Utah, were
asleep in a trailer with their 12-year-old twin
daughters. An older daughter, Carol, was asleep
in the car when the wave hit them without warning. Fearing for Carol's safety, both parents
rushed out into the swirling water. Both were carried away by the current.

Mr. Anthony Schreiver, who had started out to
frighten the bear he thought was shaking his
trailer, never reached the door. The wave hit the
camper broadside, lifted it upward, and swept it
along the river bank. End over end it tumbled.
The door popped open and water poured in. Mr.
Schreiver, nearest the door, disappeared through
the opening and into the water.

The trailer occupied by the elderly Mault couple
was also caught by the flood before anyone could
get out. It tumbled along in the water for about
200 feet before it lodged against a pile of rocks.
Inside, the water rose rapidly.

Mr. Mault pulled at the trailer door and finally, as the water reached their chins, the broken door was jerked open. As quickly as he could, he scrambled to the top of the trailer and hauled his wife up after him. The water continued to rise, so Mr. Mault pulled himself up into the limbs of an overhanging tree. Reaching down, he pulled his wife away from the clutching water.

Four times during the night the limbs to which they clung broke, dropping the elderly people back into the water. Each time, Mr. Mault scrambled back into the tree, dragging his wife after him.

None of these people realized exactly what had happened. But later, geologists were able to put together a fairly good report of the tragedy that had struck the Madison River canyon that night. The ridge that had stood across the river from the Rock Creek campground had as its base a ledge of very hard but brittle rock. On this were several hundred feet of soft rocks that had been badly worn by millions of years of being exposed to rain, snow, and ice. These soft rocks had broken into flat layers, like pages in a book. These layers were all tilted toward the river, and toward the people camped below.

The earthquake's focus was somewhere under the edge of Yellowstone National Park, so the epicenter was less than 25 miles east of the campground. The magnitude of the first shock reached 7.8 on the Richter Scale and was, therefore, among the strongest ever to hit any part of the United States. During the 24 hours that followed the first shock, 270 aftershocks were felt in the area.

The ledge upon which the ridge rested broke cleanly with the first shock. The thin layers of rock snapped and shifted a little, and then apparently settled down for a few moments. Clouds of dust rose from the ridge as the layers of rock hesitated. Then came the first of the aftershocks and the broken layers of rock tore loose from the top of the ridge.

The section of the ridge that finally broke away was 2,000 feet long, 1,300 feet wide, and 200 to 400 feet thick. It contained millions of tons of rock. As it roared down the side of the mountain it picked up speed until it hit the water of the river at nearly 100-miles-an-hour. Air and water were pushed ahead of the mass at tremendous speeds, uprooting trees, smashing cars, and hurling rocks larger than a man's head.

A large portion of the bottom of Hebgen Lake dropped suddenly. In some places, this drop was as much as 20 feet. The sudden lowering of the bottom of the lake caused huge waves to rush up and down the length of the enclosed water. At least four times in the next hour these waves struck the dam, overflowed it, and dumped tons of water into the river valley below.

But the river valley was blocked by the landslide. The force of the falling rock carried the front edge of the slide across the river, through the middle of the Rock Creek campgrounds, and more than 400 feet up the opposite side of the valley. It stopped only a few feet from the trailer, where, moments before, Polly and Hal Weston had been chatting. The slide dam was made of more than 43 million cubic yards of rock—ten times more than all of the cement used in Hoover Dam and four times larger than Grand Coulee Dam.

Standing safely on a small hill, high above the tragedy, Polly and Hal Weston and their nephews listened to the screams and calls for help that came from the darkness below them. Returning to their trailer, the four gathered up flashlights and their first aid kit.

Outside again, they stood for a moment, uncertain as to which way to go. Confusion and destruction seemed to be in all directions around them. Then they heard a man calling to them. Following his voice in the darkness, the Westons found the man.

It was Ray Painter. He lay on his back with his legs tightly pinned by a fallen pine tree. As Hal Weston worked to free him, Mr. Painter kept telling him, "Leave me alone. I'm all right! Please, please find my children!"

Polly Weston and the two boys went off into the darkness to search for Mr. Painter's family as other men joined Mr. Weston in trying to move the tree. As they made their way through the debris a battered young lady with two smaller girls approached the working men. It was Carol Painter and her sisters.

Carol had been thrown violently around inside the car when the wave smashed into it. Her head

had hit something and she was knocked unconscious for some time. When she gained consciousness, the floodwaters were going down rapidly and
she stumbled through the knee-high water to the
trailer. There she found her sisters, frightened but
unhurt, and together they had set out to find their
parents.

Freed from the fallen tree, Mr. Painter found
that he was not badly hurt, but unable to walk easily. "Leave the twins with me," he told Carol. "You
have got to find your mother."

Borrowing a flashlight, Carol again went off
into the night. A few yards away she noticed a
huddled figure. It was her mother, unconscious
but alive.

A woman and a man joined the people gathered
around Mr. Painter and his daughters. "I'm
Mildred Greene," the woman said. "I used to be
a nurse. Can I help?"

In the light from their headlights, the Greenes
had seen the water smash its way through the
camp. Then, as the water dropped lower, they saw
dozens of dazed and bleeding people crawling
over the rocks. Leaving Steve in the car, the
Greenes gathered sheets and flashlights from their
ruined tent and then worked their way down-
stream toward the landslide.

Without medical supplies there was little Mrs.
Greene could do except stop the bleeding of the
injured. She treated Mr. Painter and Carol for
shock and bandaged their cuts. Then she looked
at Mrs. Painter.

"She is badly hurt, I'm afraid," she told the men

around her. "Wrap her in a blanket and don't move her unless you have to."

The rescuers began to organize their searching efforts, scrambling over the debris in small groups, calling and shining flashlights into any pile of brush or rocks that might contain an injured person. Warren Steele was soon found alive, but badly cut and battered. Mrs. Steele was unhurt. With them were their friends, the Schreivers. Mr. Schreiver had been thrown from the trailer as it tumbled along the river bank, but somehow had managed to hang on. Finally, after the worst of the flood had passed, the trailer settled into the mud. Mrs. Schreiver had pushed Bonnie out through a broken window and then crawled through herself. Together with the Steeles, they searched through the rubble for Mrs. Schreiver's mother, Mrs. Holmes. Eventually they found her, badly hurt in the ruins of her trailer.

In another section of the valley, a group of rescuers managed to launch a boat into the rushing water. Just before dawn, five hours after the wave first struck the camp, the boatmen took the elderly Grover Mault and his wife from the limbs of their pine tree. The bodies of Purley Bennett, his little daughter, and two of his sons were also found in the piles of rocks and trees. Mrs. Bennett and 16-year-old Phillip were not found until much later in the day.

The wind that had struck the Bennett's camp had torn Phillip from his sleeping bag and thrown him into the water, where he lost consciousness.

Sometime later he awakened to find himself lying half in the now-still water. He was cold. One leg was crushed and his collarbone was broken. He dragged himself ashore and, to keep warm, dug a hole in the mud. Like a crab, he crawled into his hole and covered himself with the wet mud. There he remained, only half conscious, until dawn.

As the sun warmed Phillip, he looked around at the total destruction of what had been a pleasant holiday camp. Nearby was a woman pinned between two pine trees. She moaned weakly and tried to move. It was his mother!

Painfully, Phillip pulled himself from the mud and across the ground to her. He stayed with her for five more hours, until rescuers found them.

The problems of the survivors were not solved yet. The canyon floor began to fill with water as a lake formed behind the landslide dam. Fear that the 40-year-old Hebgen Dam might break and send another flood of water pouring suddenly down on them was also voiced by some. So, carefully carrying the injured, they moved toward higher ground. Since the roads out of the canyon were blocked by landslides in all directions, they could do nothing but wait for help.

And it came quickly. Airplanes buzzed the damaged area and then flew away. Within a few hours, they returned and men hanging from brightly colored parachutes began to drift down toward them. These were members of the famed fire fighting team known as the "Smokejumpers." These men were trained to jump into secluded areas of the mountains to fight forest fires. Now they were using their skills to help the people trapped in the Madison River valley.

Once on the ground, the Smokejumpers gave first aid to the badly injured, and using walkie-talkies, called in ambulance helicopters. Among the first to be taken out of the canyon and flown to a nearby hospital in Bozeman, Montana, were Mrs. Ray Painter and Mrs. Margaret Holmes, the elderly mother of Mrs. Schreiver. Both women died a few days later of the injuries they had received.

Amazingly, none of the 18,000 people camped inside Yellowstone National Park that night were hurt. At the Old Faithful Inn a rock chimney fell through the roof of the dining room, smashing the tables inside. But since it was nearly midnight, no one was using the room. If the quake had struck during the dinner hour, many people would have been injured or killed by the falling stones.

Some important changes had taken place under Yellowstone Park, and these caused many changes on the surface. Old Faithful Geyser became a little less prompt in its eruptions, the time between each slowing by about four minutes. Castle, Daisy, and Great Fountain geysers were found to erupt now more frequently than before. Cascade Geyser, asleep for 40 years, again became active. Economic Geyser began throwing 50-feet-high streams of water every 30 minutes—something it had not done for nearly 25 years. Grand Geyser had apparently quit forever, but a new one, named "Earthquake Geyser," appeared in Yellowstone to take its place.

Hebgen Dam had been badly damaged, either by the earthquake shock itself or by the huge waves that had smashed against it. But the cracked concrete held for nearly a year, until it could be repaired.

All around the lake were other evidences of the force of the quake. Highway 287 had slipped into the lake in four separate places. Near the town of West Yellowstone the ground split and dropped ten feet downward. This crack cut across Highway 287 and its winding path could be followed for nearly 20 miles.

The huge landslide dam across the mouth of the canyon caused some concern to the U.S. Corps of Engineers. Within a few weeks after the dam formed, the lake behind it was five miles long and 180 feet deep at the dam—nearly twice as deep as Hebgen Lake. The engineers knew that in 1925 a similar slide had blocked the Gros Ventre River some 100 miles away in Wyoming. Two years later this landslide dam had broken and the flood washed away the town of Kelly, Wyoming. Afraid that the same thing might happen here, the engineers immediately began cutting a large overflow in the landslide. This trench, 50 feet deep, allowed about half of the water to flow out of the lake and took most of the strain off the dam.

The Hebgen Lake earthquake split the earth leaving two-feet-high steps in this nearby highway.

Today, beautiful Earthquake Lake fills the lower parts of the Madison River valley and reaches almost to the repaired Hebgen Dam. It is a monument to one of the most violent earthquakes in the history of the United States and to the 19 people who lie buried beneath its dam.

CHAPTER EIGHT

AGADIR, MOROCCO FEBRUARY 29, 1960

ON THE LAST DAY OF FEBRUARY, 1960, the little Moroccan town of Agadir felt very secure. In three days, Morocco would celebrate its fifth full year of independence under the guidance of King Mohammed V. The mines high in the Atlas mountains were producing tons of phosphates and cobalt and other minerals, and more and more often these were being shipped from Agadir's deep-water port facilities. The fertile valley of the River Sous, to the south, grew more than enough fruits and vegetables to feed the 40,000 people of Agadir and provided a great deal of export trade for the harbor. The sardine fishing seemed to become better each year, and the town had become one of the country's three major fish canning centers.

Almost all of Agadir's people were Moslems and they felt certain that Allah smiled upon them as favored children. This was the third day of Ramadan, the ninth month of the Moslem calendar. Believing that the fates of men for the next year would be decided during this particular Holy Month, the faithful showed their reverence by fasting from sunrise to sunset and offering prayers far into the night.

The unusual tremors of the earth that had been felt for the last two weeks concerned no one. "Allah would not strike us while we are paying homage to his strength, omnipotence, and mercy," the Moslems said. Those who did not share this trust in Allah's mercy felt equally secure. The southwestern coast of Morocco was considered to be safe from earthquake damage, even by the insurance companies, since most of the country's quakes occurred at the opposite, eastern end of the Atlas Mountain chain.

But underlying the entire mountain range is a system of faults and two of these cross near the coastal town. Since the middle of February the rocks lying along these cracks had been shifting occasionally, moving a fraction of an inch with each slip and thereby relieving, for a brief time, the pressure against them. It wasn't until the night of February 29 that the pressure became too great.

Agadir was at that time divided into four parts, or quarters. Farthest to the west, standing on a low hill, was the Casbah. Here, surrounded by the crumbling walls of a 16th Century Portuguese fort, stood the homes of 800 to 1,000 Moslems. The homes of these people had thick walls made of sun-dried mud and this, along with the lack of windows, made them cool in the summer heat and easy to warm in the winter. Most of these houses were as old as the fort, and the adobe was dry and powdery.

Hassen ben Mohammed was just 16. He lived in the Casbah, in a two-room adobe house with his baby sister, his parents, and his grandparents. Their street was so narrow that his father could stand in the middle of it and touch the walls on both sides with his outstretched hands.

The family had just finished their evening feast which was welcomed by young Hassen after a long, unseasonably hot day. He sat at the table, quietly enjoying the feeling of a full stomach and the coolness of the night.

Hassen's father and grandfather were in the other room of the house, preparing to go to the Mosque with the other men of the neighborhood. They each put on the loose, wide trousers that the Moroccans call *serawell* and the long-tailed cotton shirts called *kumsan*. The two men came through the door just as the house began to shake. The floor seemed to ripple and Hassen's mother screamed in fright. With a crash, a large bucket that held the leftovers from the family meal fell heavily, spilling its messy contents over the swept dirt floor.

"Hassen!" the father shouted. "You know that you are to empty the pail as soon as the meal is over! If you had done as you should, that wouldn't have happened. You must stay here and clean up the floor, while your mother and grandmother do the shopping."

The two men left the house, making their way through the crowd of men moving toward the Mosque. Hassen's mother and grandmother slipped quickly into their *haiaks*, long cloaks that covered them completely, except for their eyes. As the adults left, Hassen tucked his baby sister into a bed in the corner and began to clean up the garbage that had spilled. He was never to see his parents or grandparents again.

At the base of the hill upon which the Casbah stood were two other parts of the city of Agadir. To the south, between the hill and the waterfront was a cluster of shacks made of wood and sheet iron. Here lived Moslem workers who had recently moved to the city from rural areas. The sharp shock at 10:50 frightened these simple people. Cats howled as the earth shook, and dogs ran in great circles. Feeling uncomfortable in the jumble of the city, everyone in this section bundled up what they could carry and walked quickly into the open fields around the town. Because of this, none of this group of people was killed that night.

East of the hill was another Moslem quarter, called the Talborjt. The inhabitants of the Talborjt were much like their neighbors in the Casbah. Most of the men worked in the sardine canneries or on the docks. A few were employed by the new cement factory and others worked in the nearby phosphate mines. Their houses were exactly like those of the Casbah, except that they were outside the walls of the ancient fort. Their pride was a huge Mosque with a towering minaret from which the call for prayer now sounded.

The first shock, at a little before 11 o'clock, did frighten some of the people of the Talborjt. Most of them had never felt an earthquake tremor before. But feeling certain that God would protect them, especially during Ramadan, 75 men crowded into the halls of the Mosque and knelt in prayer.

The newest, most modern part of the city stood farthest to the east. Since the end of World War II and especially in the five years since the country gained its independence, the tourist trade had become a growing source of income for Agadir. The tourist posters called the city "Agadir La Belle," ("Agadir the Beautiful") and indeed it was. Tall, modern-looking buildings lined the paved streets, and new, Western-style hotels lined the white beaches.

One of these new hotels was the four-story Hotel Saada. Room 240 was occupied by three American tourists—Sue and Jerry Martin and their baby daughter Diane. Jerry was a U.S. Air Force Lieutenant, stationed in Morocco. He and his family were spending a short leave at the sea-

side resort and had planned to leave during the
day of the 29th. But Sue had found a rug that
she wanted to buy and so they had decided to stay
over one more day in order to try to bargain with
the shop owner again.

They were glad to stay a little longer in such a
nice hotel. Their room, like all of those in the
Saada, was large and comfortable. A huge glass
door opened onto a wide balcony, and from there
the visitors could look down into lovely gardens
and see the surf throwing itself against the beach.

The first violent shock of the earthquake was
enough to rattle the doors of the hotel and tilt the
pictures on the wall. The Martins paused for a
minute or two, listening to the rattling sound. But
as it grew quiet again, they laughed at their fears,
tucked Diane in bed, and began to prepare for
their own night's rest.

The earth was quiet for nearly an hour as the
friction between the rocks on either side of the
fault below the city resisted the ever-growing pressure. Then, at 11:45, the rocks suddenly slipped
and shock waves rushed upward toward the city.

The faults that cross near Agadir are not very
far below the surface and the seismograph stations
recorded the earthquake as only a minor one. The
force of the shocks reached only 6.2 on the Richter Scale. This is only one percent as strong as the
San Francisco earthquake.

And the major shock didn't last very long. Only
about 12 seconds, which is hardly long enough for
anyone to realize what had happened. Yet to

A large sign in English and Arabic stands above the wreckage of the modern Saada Hotel. The Saada, which means happiness, was destroyed by the 1960 earthquake that took several thousand lives in the resort town of Agadir.

those who experienced it, this short period of time must have seemed like an eternity. It began quietly and slowly, the shivering of the earth and the growling that seemed to come from everywhere increasing steadily as the rocks slipped. "An animal, snarling as it tried to shake us off its back," is the way it was later described.

It was during the sixth second that all of the damage was done. During that very short time period the earth under Agadir suddenly leapt sideways about four feet and then, like a rubber band that had been stretched, snapped back again. "The earth was kicked out from under us," said one survivor.

In the Casbah, adobe walls crumbled into dust and roof tiles shattered against the ground like bombs. Of the 800 or more people who were within the walls of the old fort that evening, only 50 were alive the next morning. Two of these were Hassen ben Mohammed and his sister. The bodies of his parents and his grandparents were buried in the rubble and, if they were found, they were never identified.

Below the Casbah, in the Talborjt, it was the Mosque that was the hardest hit. First the roof and then the stone walls of the building crashed downward onto the backs of the praying men inside. Only the minaret was left standing.

Sue Martin was in the bathroom at 11:45. Her husband and daughter were in the bedroom. The wrenching shock broke the hotel's foundations and the entire building settled straight downward. Mrs. Martin later reported that she heard a rumble and "then everything dropped. It was like going down in a fast elevator." In the pitch darkness, she heard Diane crying. Then her husband called, "I've found Diane!"

"I'm trapped," Sue called. "I can't move my legs or one arm."

But only silence answered her.

Similar cries for help came from the trapped and injured all over the city. But there were few who were able to help. Three companies of the

Royal Moroccan Army were stationed in the town, but most of the men were in the barracks when they collapsed and almost every man was either killed or badly injured. The local police barracks were not damaged, but most of the policemen were on leave for the Ramadan celebration and were killed in the ruins of the city. Hospitals, without lights or water, were hard pressed to take care of the patients already there.

Fortunately, however, the destruction was not very widespread, perhaps because the focus of the earthquake was so near to the surface. Only two and a half miles away from Agadir was a French-Moroccan airbase, and it was undamaged. Rescue teams set out immediately for the stricken town. The French aircraft carrier *La Fayette* was ordered into the area and by dawn her planes were flying over the town. "The city looks as if a giant foot had stepped on it and squashed it flat," came back the first report. Trucks carrying stretchers and fire-fighting equipment arrived on the scene and the digging began with the rising sun.

The unseasonable heat wave continued. During the early afternoon of March 1, the temperature reached 105°. The faithful Moslems, struggling with the heavy ruins, refused food and even water as they worked, in strict observance of Ramadan. Many of the injured refused to take medicine until after sunset for fear that this would break the Holy Commandments.

At about six o'clock in the afternoon, 18 hours after the collapse of the Hotel Saada, a detachment of French Marines was digging in the ruins. Pausing to rest, they heard a faint voice, calling out in English. Their officer, Lieutenant Montus, spoke a few words of English and answered the calls. A brief search revealed Jerry Martin and his daughter Diane, who were both dug from the rubble alive. Sue Martin remained buried in the wreckage, but they could hear her voice. Lieutenant Montus assured Sue her family was uninjured.

Hour after hour, the Marines dug into the pile of debris that had been Agadir's most modern hotel. Montus kept up a constant conversation with the buried woman, both in order to keep her spirits up and to give his workmen a direction in which to dig. The night turned cold and then colder still as the men worked. Down through the roof they cut, then through the shattered fourth floor, and carefully through the rubble filling the third floor. Always they dug toward the voice.

Gently removing the rubble, a stone at a time, the diggers found Sue's feet. But they were unable to pull her free. A doctor who was working nearby was called. He felt the woman's feet and found a faint pulse in her ankle. "She will not live another hour," he decided.

But the French lieutenant was not going to give up. As the walls of the deep shaft threatened to collapse on the men, he ordered hot water to be poured into empty wine bottles and placed these around Sue's nearly frozen feet. Then the digging crew was ordered back to the top of the smashed hotel and a second shaft was begun.

By mid-morning of March second, the second shaft had reached Sue's head. A rubber tube was slipped into her mouth and she was able to drink water for the first time in nearly 30 hours. As the afternoon sun blazed down on them, the workmen managed to enlarge the shafts to the point that they could get car jacks under the door that lay across the woman. And finally, at about three o'clock in the afternoon of March second, Sue Martin was carefully lifted from the ruined hotel that had buried her alive for almost 40 hours.

On March third planes from U.S. bases in Germany arrived, bringing 300 men, bulldozers, food, medicine, and portable operating rooms. Hundreds of injured were dug from the ruins each day, and every available airplane was used to fly them to Casablanca and Rabat. Many died on the way and many more were found already dead in the rubble.

By this time, however, other problems were beginning to appear. First, it was the heat, which made it difficult to work long hours. Then the thousands of bodies still buried in the ruins began to rot, and the possibility of plague spreading among the rescuers became a danger. The animals also presented a problem—millions of rats from the collapsed sewers, chased by dogs and cats that no longer had homes. Jackals and vultures were drawn by the smell of rotting flesh. Rabies, typhoid fever, cholera, epidemic typhus, and tetanus constantly threatened both the rescuers and the survivors.

The king's son, who had been appointed the job of directing the work at Agadir, had to face a terrible decision. Perhaps as many as 10,000 people still lay buried in the remains of the city. Some of them might still be alive. But the threat of disease that hung over the rescuers was becoming too great.

On March fifth the town was officially abandoned. The more than 15,000 people who had survived the earthquake were moved to a city of tents farther up the coast. Everyone was vaccinated and helicopters sprayed the ruins with DDT.

The town was divided into ten sectors and teams of men wearing gas masks and gloves moved in. American bulldozers plowed through the rubble, smashing still-standing walls and leveling the debris. Teams of men on foot, carrying shovels, made one last search of the ruins just ahead of the bulldozers. They found a total of 21 people, all alive but buried, before the huge machines could crush them.

Other bulldozers were kept busy burying the dead. Huge trenches, two feet deep, ten feet wide, and hundreds of feet long, were gouged out. The bodies were carefully laid in these trenches, covered with quicklime and DDT, and then buried with tons of dirt. Many of these people remain unidentified.

On March 15, the harbor was opened again to shipping, and tons of supplies began to flow into the dead city.

King Mohammed V and his son pledged their personal fortunes to help rebuild the city and told the people of Agadir that on March second, 1961, one year after the disaster, they would come and inaugurate the new city. But by that date the ruins of the totally destroyed city had not yet been completely cleared, and more than $1,500,000 had been spent.

But Agadir still lives. The new city is slowly rebuilding itself and someday, perhaps, it will again become "Agadir La Belle."

CHAPTER NINE

CHILE 1960

TWO HUNDRED YEARS AGO AND MORE, the early scientists who studied the earth believed that the mountains of the earth's surface had been created suddenly during some tremendous catastrophe. Fiords and other evidences of land that has dropped downward were explained in the same way. This theory of early geologists was called the Theory of Catastrophism.

But about the beginning of the Nineteenth Century it was discovered that even the hardest, most brittle rocks would bend and flow if they were put under great enough pressure for a very long period of time. With this discovery, the Theory of Catastrophism became unpopular. Modern geologists think that folds in the rocks of the earth have taken place very slowly, over thousands and thousands of years.

With the invention of better measuring instruments, the idea that the surface of the earth can change very slowly was proven. The most rapidly rising areas of the world have been found to be in Scandinavia, where large regions are rising at a rate of about one-half inch per year. And a part of the Netherlands has been found to be sinking by one inch every 25 years.

Earthquakes, of course, are catastrophes that suddenly push up a part of the earth's surface or cause another part to drop. Sometimes they cause the earth to shift sideways along a crack in the surface. But these almost always change only a very small part of the earth. Land lying along the San Andreas Fault in California has been known to suddenly shift northward as much as 23 feet. In 1899, 1,000 square miles of Alaska were suddenly tilted upward. One place was 15 feet higher than it had been. And the 1964 quake in the same state caused 22,000 square miles of the earth's surface to sink an average of five and one-half feet.

Another land area changed by such a catastrophe was the coast of Chile. Here, during the month between May 21 and June 22, 1960, nearly 5,000 square miles of coastline dropped approximately six feet. This stretch of land, 12 to 18 miles wide and 300 miles long, sank as a result of the slipping of the earth's crust along a fault that lay somewhere under the water of the Pacific, parallel to the beach. Just how much land settled downward is not known exactly, since part of it lies deep underwater.

Earthquakes shake some part of the earth almost every minute. But only a few of these are strong enough for people to feel and it is an unusually bad year when more than 20 earthquakes with magnitudes of more than 7 occur. These figures show how severe the series of quakes that struck the coast of Chile in 1960 really were. During the 32 days that the earth shook, a total of 225 tremors were felt. Of these, ten had magnitudes of between 7 and 8, and three were recorded as being above 8.

Chile lies within the earthquake belt that surrounds the Pacific Ocean and in which 80 percent of the world's earthquakes occur. So the people who live there have learned to expect the earth to tremble under their feet once in a while, and even to expect to suffer some damage occasionally.

In 1939 earthquakes badly damaged the cities of Chillán and Concepción. At that time, the government began to require that buildings be built in such a way as to be earthquake-proof. All new buildings were to be built on firm, solid ground and never on loose soil washed into an area by water or used to fill in low regions. Wood should be used for smaller buildings and reinforced concrete for taller buildings. All parts of the buildings should be tightly fastened together and decorations such as cornices and eaves should be kept small. Rules were set up to regulate the distance between upright supports and the heights that chimneys could be built.

But people tend to forget how damaging a really bad earthquake can be, so many of the buildings of Chile were not as well built as they should have been. In many of the larger cities, where houses had been built on fill land, as much as 80 percent of the buildings were totally destroyed by the first shocks. Outside the larger cities, however, the damage was much less. Most of the villages, even those along the coast, consisted of wooden houses built on solid rock.

The 1960 earthquakes began south of Concepción. The epicenter of the first shocks was on the peninsula of Arauco. It was early morning, Saturday, May 21. Since May is a winter month south of the equator, it was still dark at six a.m. A shock with a magnitude of 7.75 struck the area, but only a few people were killed by falling chimneys and the damage generally was not very bad.

Even though the magnitude of the shock was great, the intensity was not. That is, the amount of energy that reached the surface was not as high as you might expect from an earthquake of such high magnitude. Because of this, it is assumed that the focus of the earthquake was very, very deep in the earth. Perhaps the fault that caused this first shock lies 40 miles or more beneath the surface.

The earthquake-wise people of the area moved quickly out of their houses, looking for open country that would be far away from falling buildings. Half an hour later, still before sunrise, a second shock as strong as the first hit. But no one died even though there was further damage to property. This second shock can be called an "aftershock," since it came from the same focus as the first earthquake.

The next 33 hours were calm, and the people of Concepción and the towns on the Arauco Peninsula began to relax. Sunday, May 22, was a beautiful day. The weather was warm for that time of year and the sun shone brightly for what the Chileans knew might be the last time until Spring. So, when the shocks began again at mid-afternoon, most of the people were out-of-doors. Many of those who were near buildings moved to safety as several small shudders ran through the earth. Because of these fortunate circumstances, when the major shock came at about three o'clock, there were fewer deaths than there might have been.

This shock was caused by rocks slipping along a fault that lay several miles south of the focus of the first quake. The epicenter of this quake was at sea but near the coast, just south of the Arauco Peninsula. The slipping rocks produced a tremendous amount of energy, registering a magnitude of 8.5. This shows a magnitude almost ten times that of the first shocks of the day before.

The entire southern half of the South American Continent quivered, and in southern Chile homes and buildings everywhere collapsed. In seconds, 60,000 homes tumbled into rubble. Dozens of factories, office buildings, hotels, churches, and schools crumpled like paper. If this had not been a Sunday afternoon, or if the usual cold rain of winter had been falling, the death toll would have run into the hundreds of thousands.

There were two faults involved in the series of earthquakes that followed. One lies parallel to the coast, with its northern end under the Arauco Peninsula. The second, smaller fault lies far inland in what is known as the lakes region of Chile. This fault, like its larger sister, runs almost due north and south.

The next day, Monday, the rains and cold weather returned and so did the earthquakes. During the next week at least three more sections of the long fault under the ocean gave way. These were farther south, down the coast from Arauco, and all of the towns and villages along the coast between Puerto Saavedra and Island Chiloé suffered severe damage. The rocks along the inland fault under the lakes region slipped again and again. Thousands of landslides blocked roads and dammed rivers. Casualties in both areas were high.

The land that suffered the most in both areas was loose, silty soil that had become water saturated. With the almost-constant shaking, this soil became even more liquid. A car, which had been left standing on solid ground, sank straight down into the fluid soil. In Puerto Montt a river of sand flowed into the harbor and surrounded a ship anchored there. Later, when the sand settled, the ship was unable to move. Its owners finally turned it into a hotel.

As was mentioned earlier in this chapter, 5,000 square miles of Chile's coastline sank as the fault offshore gave way. Before the earthquake, Valdivia had been a freshwater port, many miles upriver from the coast. Now saltwater from the ocean covers many miles of land inland from the town. But not all of the coastline sank. The western side of Arauco Peninsula lifted upward four feet and the island of Mocha which was just southwest of the epicenter of the main shock was raised seven feet.

Inland, the volcano Ruyehue began to erupt. Not since 1905 had this mountain been so violent. For several weeks, lava flowed from its sides and pillars of ash towered 20,000 feet into the sky.

Rescuers dug carefully through the damp rubble, constantly afraid that a new series of shocks would collapse the ruined walls and shafts on them. Survivors camped uncomfortably in the open, preferring the rain and cold to the probable dangers of further earthquakes.

With all of the major roads and railroad beds torn apart by the heaving earth, with all minor roads closed because of the rain and hundreds of landslides, and with all of the harbors flooded and destroyed when the land upon which they stood suddenly sank, the only way to get help to the people of the stricken area was by air. Fifty-four U.S. Air Force planes airlifted two 400-bed field hospitals into the disaster area. Serum, water purifiers, blankets, clothing, food, and men were constantly being unloaded at the few undamaged airfields.

At the end of that terrible month, no one was certain exactly how many people were dead. One estimate said 6,000. One hundred thirty thousand homes were completely destroyed and most of the region's larger buildings were badly damaged. Total property damage was estimated to be as high as half a billion dollars, which was nearly five percent of the total wealth of the entire country.

Massive aid was needed, and most of the countries of the world responded quickly. The Import-Export Bank of Washington, D.C., immediately loaned the Chilean government ten million dollars. West Germany offered to take over the rebuilding of the city of Valdivia, which has a large number of citizens of German descent. Argentina took responsibility for the island of Chiloé, while Sweden adopted Puerto Saavedra.

The destruction caused by the sudden slipping of the earth off the coast of Chile was more widespread than just this. The rapid drop of the ocean's floor, and perhaps underwater landslides caused by the earthquake, created a series of tsunamis that killed people 10,000 miles away from Chile.

The waves were created just offshore and rushed out in all directions at speeds of more than 400 miles-an-hour. They washed away 630 of the 800 people living in the fishing village of Queilén. The entire village of Queule was lost to the water and 35 people disappeared along with their homes.

In the Chilean port of Corral approximately 80 people died in the waves. The first was a "smooth wave" during which the water rose, swiftly but gently until it was 15 feet higher than normal. There it stood quietly for a few moments and then suddenly withdrew with a "kind of metallic sucking noise." A sandbank, normally ten feet under the surface of the water, was clearly seen in the middle of the harbor. The water remained out for perhaps 20 minutes and then returned as a wall, 26 feet high and traveling more than 100 miles-an-hour. Within a few seconds, it smashed 800 homes and heaped them all together in a pile at the foot of a hill. After ten or 15 minutes, the water again retreated with the same metallic sucking noise. A third wave, even higher than the previous one, smashed ashore an hour later, but there was nothing left for it to destroy.

Tsunamis often follow earthquakes, especially if the focus of the quake is under the ocean. It is impossible to predict when these dangerous waves will be produced and so the villages along the coast of Chile could not be warned. But the rest of the world had plenty of warning of their coming.

In 1946, after 165 Hawaiians were killed by a tsunami, the U.S. Coast and Geodetic Survey established the Seismic Sea Wave Warning System. Centered at Honolulu, Hawaii, the system is made up of ten earthquake-recording stations and 20

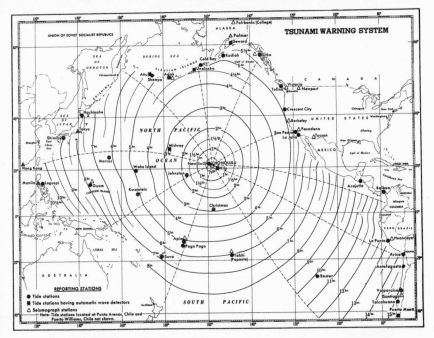

This map shows the extensive tsunami warning system in the Pacific Ocean—giving locations of earthquake-recording and wave-measuring stations. (See key) Also indicated by the concentric circles is an estimated travel time of a tsunami, or sea wave, that probably originated off the coast of Chile and struck Honolulu 15 hours later.

wave-measuring stations scattered around the Pacific Ocean. Twelve hours before the first wave struck the islands, the Hawaiians were warned of its possible approach. Five and a half hours before the water smashed ashore, the people were told that it was certain that a tsunami would hit Hawaii around midnight.

For 16 hours after the earthquake, the waves rushed outward across the Pacific. Their crests were only two or three feet high in the deep, open ocean and the crews of passing ships barely noticed them at all. But when the increased amount of water reached the gentle underwater slopes that lie offshore from the city of Hilo, it built up into huge walls of water. One after another, at least three such waves smashed at Hilo and the beaches around it. The first wave was only four feet high and did no damage. The second was nine feet above average high tide and could not cross the seawall that protected the city and its harbor. But the third wave crested at 35 feet, and smashed across the seawall and into the city itself. Docks and piers were crushed; homes and hotels were demolished. But because of the early warnings, most of the buildings and streets were empty. The damage to property amounted to $50 million, and 61 people who hadn't believed the warnings died that night in Hawaii.

The warning had been sent on ahead of the waves to all parts of the Pacific. Japan received the warning at least five times, and knew about the damage at Hilo nearly nine hours before the tsunamis hit the islands of Hondo and Hokkaido. But, for some unknown reason, the warning was not spread to the thousands of fishermen and rice farmers living along Japan's coast. After traveling over 10,000 miles for 25 hours, the 20-foot-high tsunamis wiped the beaches of northern Japan clean. Five thousand homes were washed away, 190 people drowned, and 50,000 were homeless.

Evidently, just being able to predict a tsunami is not enough. People have to be organized in such a way that they can warn each other.

CHAPTER TEN

ALASKA
MARCH 27, 1964

GOOD FRIDAY, 1964, had been a beautiful day in the part of Alaska that borders on Prince William Sound. The temperature in Anchorage that afternoon reached a point only a few degrees below freezing, and the air was crisp with the gentle fall of powdery snow. At 5:30 in the evening, holiday shoppers crowded the streets. Some thought about the Easter clothes they had bought. Others thought of the eggs to be dyed. Some, perhaps, dreamed of the early spring the warmer weather promised. Surely no one recalled St. Matthew's description of the first Good Friday, "And, behold . . . the earth did quake, and the rocks rent."

But 150 miles to the southeast of Anchorage and 12 miles below the blue waters of Prince William Sound the earth was not as quiet and calm as it seemed on the surface. The rocks lying along an ancient fault had managed to hold together in spite of the pressures that had pushed against them for many years. But these pressures had continued until now the breaking point had been reached. Suddenly, without warning, there were shocks that could be felt on the surface; the rocks along the fault shifted. One side apparently moved upward while the other slipped down. Between 5:36 and 5:41—five short minutes—200,000 megatons of energy were released. This was about the same amount of energy that would be released if 200 *billion* tons of TNT were to explode all at once. It would take a thousand or more hydrogen bombs to produce this much energy.

At thousands of miles-per-hour, the shock waves rushed toward the surface where half of Alaska's 250,000 people unknowingly waited for disaster. Within these five short minutes 115 of them were to die and 4,500 were to be left homeless. The property damage finally was to total $750,000,000—nearly 100 times what it had cost to buy the entire territory from Russia a century before.

Seismographs all over the world began to record the violent shocks which were to reach 8.5 on the Richter Scale, the highest reading of any earthquake to strike North America in 65 years. But perhaps the first person to "see" the quake was a late shopper in the J. C. Penney store in Anchorage. Admiring several small porcelain figurines, Mrs. Carol Tucker was nearly alone on the third floor of the new, five-story, windowless store. Suddenly, the tiny figures began to dance gently on the glass counter top. Sensing that something was seriously wrong, rather than understanding what was actually happening, Mrs. Tucker walked rapidly toward the escalator. She could feel the entire building shaking, as the dolls had done moments before, and realized that an earthquake had begun. Then, without a warning flicker, the power failed and she was plunged into total darkness.

Now thoroughly frightened, she stumbled along in the dark to the stalled escalator and felt her way as quickly as possible down the shivering metal steps. Heavy objects crashed around her, unseen in the dark. With her arms over her head, she stumbled over the floor that was buckling and weaving as if it were alive. Falling once, badly tearing a ligament in her leg, she finally reached the ground floor. There she could see daylight flowing through the glass display windows that lined the front of the store. With relief, she made her way across the rippling floor to the front door of the store and looked out onto the intersection of 5th Avenue and D Street. There she stopped, watching with shock as a car bounced down the street, its tires sometimes two feet off the ground and its rear fishtailing as its driver desperately tried to control the vehicle. As she stood there,

The marquee of the Denali Theater
was level with the sidewalk after the ground
beneath the theater dropped nearly
ten feet during an earthquake.

This sidewalk on 4th Street
in Anchorage, Alaska, was broken apart
in 1964 by earthquake shocks.

clutching the trembling door frame, the concrete facade of the store broke loose and crashed to the sidewalk in front of her. A man on the sidewalk disappeared under tons of concrete. The bouncing car was hit by one huge slab, fatally injuring its driver. A parked car was later to be dug from the rubble, crushed until it was only 18 inches thick.

A block north, on 4th Street, the shock waves seemed to cut the ground out from under the buildings standing on the north side of the street, leaving the south side untouched. The old Denali Theater dropped nearly ten feet into the ground and finally settled with its nearly undamaged marquee level with the sidewalk.

At the Anchorage International Airport the control tower shuddered with the shock and finally toppled, killing the air traffic controller who was on duty there. The Presbyterian Hospital was left without water, heat, or electricity and patients were treated by doctors and nurses carrying flashlights. Bouquets of Easter flowers were left standing in the lightly falling snow as the florist shop's front crumbled into dust.

Suburban Turn-Again-By-The-Sea was a pleasant residential community of about 300 homes. Many of these stood near the cliff that overlooked Cook Inlet. At the first shock, many of the residents of these houses rushed out to escape the collapsing roofs only to be flung to the ground by sharper jolts. Fissures suddenly opened around them, and then the entire bluff slipped downward toward the churning water below.

But Anchorage was lucky. Although 75 percent of its property was damaged or destroyed, only nine people were killed in that terrible five minutes. But other towns were not so lucky.

About 125 miles due east of Anchorage, at the head of a fiord overlooking Prince William Sound, stands the old gold camp of Valdez. The towering mountains seem to be trying to push the little village into the water, and the steep-roofed houses crowd around the deep-water harbor. Nearly 1,200 people lived here that Good Friday and many of them were at the harbor at 5:36, watching the unloading of the 400-foot steamship *Chena*.

This quaint little town, sometimes called the "Switzerland of Alaska," was built on loose, silty soil that had been deposited centuries ago by a retreating glacier. A small river flowed across this silt and washed much of it into the fiord. It was on this unstable base that the people of Valdez had built a 100-foot-long pier. The water alongside the pier was deep and the *Chena* was able to unload her cargo directly onto the wooden pier. It was an exciting event to the children of the town and they liked to stand along the sides of the pier in order to see better. This day, being a holiday, and such a beautiful day, many parents also stood on the pier to watch the unloading activities and to chat with each other. Counting the dockworkers who were working the ship, 28 people crowded together near the end of the wooden dock.

No one is exactly certain what happened as the quake's shock waves hit the town. Fissures three feet wide opened up in the soft soil under the town. Houses and buildings collapsed as the loose material upon which they were built shifted. And then, almost immediately, the wave hit the pier.

Some of the people who were on higher ground reported that the water simply rose quickly. Others said that they saw a "wall of water" rush up the fiord. Whatever the case, the sudden onrush of water cut the silt from under the pier. The people who had, moments before, been enjoying their free day, began to run. But before any of them reached the end of the pier, the wooden structure collapsed and all 28 people were caught by the receding water and washed out into the sea.

The people on the island of Kodiak had more warning of the coming wave, since Kodiak is more than 200 miles to the southwest of the earthquake's epicenter. The shock waves were felt all over the island. One man reported that it felt like he "was walking on Jello." The Fleet Weather Station warned of a possible tsunami, and so there was little loss of life.

Some people believe that the animals of Kodiak knew that the earthquake was coming long before humans could feel it. The huge Kodiak bears, for which the island is named, left hibernation two weeks earlier than usual—the day before the quake. Their tracks showed that instead of wandering aimlessly around as you might expect a sleepy bear to do, these bears left their caves and dens on the dead run. Even the domesticated cattle seemed to sense something wrong, and several herds moved high up into the hills earlier than usual.

The first wave was a gradual one, gently flowing in for a while, then gently flowing out. It hit Kodiak at 6:47, more than an hour after the first shock of the earthquake. The quiet, nondestructive first wave warned those people near the beach that the Weather Service warning had been an accurate one.

The second wave was a 30-foot-high wall of water that smashed ashore a few minutes later. It rushed across the harbor, crushing piers and docks, tearing ships loose from their anchors and hurling them into the heart of town. Kraft's General Store is reported to have been lifted from its foundations and floated out to sea, only to float back again on the next wave, then sail back out to sea once more and again be safely returned to shore. Finally it settled on dry land only a few yards from its original foundations.

Down the coast from the town of Kodiak stood the Aleut village of Kagayak. With the first wave, all 41 of the villagers moved to higher ground. After the second wave, a small party of villagers tried to return to their homes to salvage food and other belongings. An hour after the second wave had receded, the third and largest wave crushed the village. Six of the Indians tried to ride out the wave in a small boat. Three were washed overboard.

The third wave did even more damage at Kodiak. The 131-ton crab boat *Selief* was picked up like a cork and dumped ashore. An hour later, the fourth wave floated the boat back into the harbor. Throughout the night, wave followed wave, with only about an hour between each. Dawn on March 28 revealed a ruined island. Only the three Aleuts were dead, but more than half of the fishing fleet was gone or damaged badly, and the canning industry was almost a total loss.

Perhaps it was the little town of Seward, only a few miles west of the epicenter, that received the hardest blow from the Good Friday earthquake. Perched on the upper end of Resurrection Bay, a short distance from the Gulf of Alaska, Seward and its 1,700 people were important to the economy of the state. Its deep-water port remains free of ice all winter and tons of cargo cross the docks. From here, oil, food, and other necessities for surviving the long winter are shipped inland by rail and by truck.

But the land upon which Seward's waterfront facilities were built was very much like that of Valdez. Streams flowing out of the mountains had washed gravel, sand, and silt into Resurrection Bay. Settling to the bottom, this loose soil formed a steep slope of between 30 and 40 degrees. It was into this uncertain base that the piling of the piers had been driven and upon which many of the warehouses and other buildings of the waterfront had been built. Texaco and Standard Oil Companies had built 16 storage tanks on the same type of soil, and on Good Friday these tanks contained 40,000 barrels of petroleum products.

A ship and buoy were washed up across this road in Seward, Alaska, by a tsunami.

Nevertheless, the people of Seward were proud of their town. They sponsored an annual salmon fishing competition that had become world famous. They worked hard to blend their city and its industry into the natural beauty of their surroundings. They built parks and libraries and supported their excellent schools. As a result of all this work, Seward had been notified that it had been selected to receive an All American City Award. The ceremony in which this award was scheduled to be presented was to take place one week after Easter.

With the first shocks, nearly a mile of waterfront slipped into the bay. Docks and piers collapsed as the loose soil under them slid down the steep underwater slope. Undercut by this landslide, all eight of the Standard Oil Company's storage tanks collapsed, pouring thousands of gallons of oil and gasoline into the harbor. At about the same time, the eight Texaco tanks exploded one after another, each with a tremendous roar that drowned out the growling of the earth. Orange flames spread rapidly in all directions as the burning oil ran across the ground and into the sea.

As the first sea wave struck the harbor, the oil-covered water itself burst into flame. Pilings, that had been snapped off by the force of the tsunami, floated upright because their bases were waterlogged, and their tops blazed like torches in the water.

No one really knows when the fires finally burned out. Everyone in the ruined town was busy trying to stay alive as wave after wave, six in all,

smashed across what had been the four-million-
dollar harbor. High school student Linda McRae
saw the first wave as it crossed the bay. Quickly,
she gathered up her three-week-old nephew and,
along with her brother, ran to the back of a
neighbor's house. Scrambling in desperation over
empty oil barrels, they climbed first onto the roof
of a garage and then to the top of the house.

Within seconds, the wave hit the garage, breaking it into splinters. Beneath them, the porch of
the house washed away, and then parts of the
house itself. Finally, the portion of the house to
which the three people clung floated free from its
foundation and swirled off into the darkness.
Linda remembers seeing the raging fire and won-
dering whether it would eventually reach their
bobbing raft.

Battered by floating debris, the remains of the
house finally came to rest against four large trees.
There the three lucky survivors rode out the rest
of the waves and finally, as the water receded,
managed to lower themselves into the ruined
house.

So far as human deaths were concerned, Seward
was fairly lucky. Thirteen of its citizens were
killed. Nearby, in the Aleut village called Chenega,
the death toll was almost double that of Seward.
Chenega had been a cluster of 20 houses, each
standing on high pilings. The force of the waves
cut these pilings down to the level of the sand and
carried off all of the houses. Along with the debris
went the bodies of ten adults and 13 children.

It was the property damage in Seward that was so terrible. The docks were gone. The canneries and oil storage areas lay in total ruin. Both the railroad and the highway to Anchorage were cut in dozens of places. The power plant and water treatment plant were both damaged and useless. Cut off, except by air, the citizens of Seward had to take care of themselves as they began to repair the damage of the worst earthquake the United States has suffered in this century.

The full extent of the force of this earthquake was not realized until later. Geologists immediately began a careful survey of the damaged area and discovered that over a million square miles of the earth's surface had been affected in some way.

The earthquake, fires, and tsunami that struck Alaska on Good Friday, 1964, took many lives and caused property damage that finally totalled $750,000,000.

CHAPTER ELEVEN

THE
TREMBLING
EARTH

WE ARE USED TO CHANGES around us. Our friends grow taller and older. The weather and the seasons do not remain the same. Moving water changes the shape of our beaches and river banks. But we like to think that the ground upon which we walk is stable and unchanging.

Each year, however, this "solid" ground trembles, heaves, and cracks hundreds of thousands of times. The best buildings man can build sway and sometimes even crumble while thousands of people die. Cries of "EARTHQUAKE" flash around the world as the earth suddenly changes beneath our feet, leaving us fearful of the unknown.

It is difficult to estimate the damage caused by a major earthquake. The shivering of the ground can be felt over a million square miles of the earth's surface. Loose soil shifts and buildings that are not anchored on solid rock can collapse. The surface of the earth can crack open in huge fissures that often run for miles, cutting through houses, highways, and railroad tracks, tearing them apart. Fissures and the shaking earth can break gas and water lines while uncontrollable fires often add to the damage of the earthquake. Unstable soil and rocks that happen to be perched on the side of steep hills can shake loose and come crashing down as a landslide, crushing everything below under tons of debris.

But almost as bad as the damage caused directly by the earthquake is the destruction caused by huge sea waves, called *tsunamis*. If the earthquake occurs under the sea, the ocean floor may be suddenly disturbed. This usually causes a series of waves to travel rapidly through the water in all directions, very similar to what happens when you throw a rock into a quiet pond. These tsunamis, however, move across the surface of the ocean at tremendous speeds—sometimes at 500 miles-per-hour. Where the water is deep, the waves are low and commonly pass unnoticed under a large ship at sea. But when the tsunamis enter shallow water, the height of the waves begins to build up. Where the shore is particularly shallow, these waves smash across the beach as a wall of water that can be taller than a ten-story building. So it is possible for an earthquake to kill people and destroy property thousands of miles away within a few hours.

People who live along the edge of the sea near the center of the earthquake's disturbance will have little chance to escape the swiftly moving waves. But, thanks to the Seismic Sea Wave Warning System, warnings of possible tsunamis can be sent out to people living far from the earthquake area. Ten earthquake-recording stations and 20 wave-measuring stations have been built in various parts of the Pacific Ocean. When these instruments record a quake on the ocean floor and tsunamis spreading out from it, a warning is sent by radio to the governments of those countries likely to be hit. With several hours' notice, it is usually possible to move people away from the beaches. Many lives have been saved by this system.

If an earthquake happens to occur beneath a heavily populated area, the damage to property may be very great. But the most terrible destruction of earthquakes is the number of human lives that is sometimes taken. You have read about some of the most deadly earthquakes in this book. It is often impossible to determine exactly how many people are killed in these catastrophes, particularly if they occurred many years ago, or in countries today whose census figures are inaccurate. Some people estimate that as many as 60,000 people died as a result of the earthquake in Lisbon, Portugal in 1755. At least 100,000 people were killed by the quake that destroyed Messina, Italy in 1908. Perhaps 140,000 human beings died in 1923 when an earthquake struck the Kwanto Plain of Japan. And at least 100,000 people were killed in the 1960 catastrophe at Agadir, Morocco. And these terrible stories are only a small sample of the total death toll caused by earthquakes during the history of man. During the last 1,000 years or so there have been at least two dozen earthquakes that have each killed 50,000 or more people.

Earthquakes can and do occur in almost all parts of the world. But they strike most often near the younger mountain ranges of the world. Only a few of the major earthquakes that have occurred during the time man has been writing his history were outside the two great earthquake belts that follow these mountain ranges.

One circles the Pacific Ocean. The other follows the high mountains from Portugal to Burma. Many less dangerous earthquakes occur in the region of the Mid-Atlantic Ridge, a range of mountains that runs down the center of the Atlantic Ocean.

These belts where earthquakes most often occur are almost the same as those in which the most active volcanoes now stand. But we cannot assume that earthquakes are caused by volcanoes. The violent explosion of a volcano may cause the earth to shake and crack, but these "quakes" are very small when compared to a major earthquake.

Geologists, scientists who study the earth, use the word "earthquake" to name what happens when rocks slip suddenly along a crack in the earth. A crack along which the rocks have slipped is called a *fault*. The rocks may move up or down along the fault, or they may move sideways.

On the surface, or deep in the earth where the rocks actually slip along the fault, is a zone called the *focus* of the earthquake. The focus may be confined to a small area, or it may extend for miles along the fault. The focus may be on the surface of the earth and after the earthquake we may be able to see the fault running through the rocks. But most often, the focus of the earthquake is beneath the surface of the earth—generally within about 50 miles of the surface. A few earthquakes, however, will have their focuses several hundreds of miles deep.

If the focus of the earthquake is below the surface of the earth, the waves it produces rush out in all directions. If the earthquake is powerful, these waves may affect the surface of the earth for many miles around. The worst shaking, however, will usually occur on the surface of the earth directly above the focus. This region on the surface, closest to the focus, is called the *epicenter* of the earthquake. It is here that most of the destruction usually takes place.

When the epicenter of an earthquake is near a populated area, scientists and building engineers usually study its effects carefully. They talk to the people who survived to try to find out what they felt; the engineers study buildings and other man-made structures, and they look carefully at the changes that have taken place in the ground.

Using this information, the scientists and engineers can determine the *intensity* of the earthquake. The intensity of an earthquake does not tell us how strong the earthquake was. It only tells us what effects the earthquake had on a certain area. So, intensity is a measure of the power of the earthquake determined from observing man-made structures and the earth's movements or cracks.

These effects, however, do not always tell much about the strength of the earthquake. How deep the focus of the earthquake is will have a lot to do with how extensive the earthquake is. A powerful earthquake whose focus is very, very deep may do less damage than one that is much weaker but whose focus is closer to the surface. For example, the earthquake that destroyed Agadir, Morocco in 1960 and killed 100,000 people was only about 1/100 as strong as the 1923 earthquake in Japan, but its focus was closer to the surface.

The conditions of the surface above the focus—the epicenter—also may cause a weaker earthquake to result in more damage than a stronger one would have elsewhere. A strong quake whose focus is under the ocean or under an uninhabited area may have little effect on a populated area of the earth. Or if the earthquake takes place under a region of solid rock or of tightly packed, dry soil the damage at the epicenter may not be very great. On the other hand, certain types of soil that seem quite solid even when they are wet may turn "soupy" when they are shaken by an earthquake. And the result may be tremendous damage to the buildings constructed on them.

The strength of an earthquake is known as its *magnitude*. Hundreds of *seismograph* instruments around the world constantly wait for the earth to shake. These instruments record the magnitude of each of the million or so quakes that occur each year. These records are quickly sent to thousands of scientists around the world and, with the help of computers, these men and women work together to find the location of each earthquake's epicenter, focus, and magnitude. Within minutes after the earthquake strikes, and often long before the survivors can send out word of the disaster, help and warnings of possible tsunamis may be on their way.

The scientific study of earthquakes has also shown engineers and builders how to construct buildings that can better withstand the shocks of earthquakes. Learning how to do this has not been an easy job, and is not yet complete. Scientists and engineers from almost every country in the world are now working together to solve this important problem.

It is fairly easy to build a building that must simply hold up under its own weight and the weight of its contents. These weights are pulled straight down by gravity and can be measured easily. And it is fairly easy to experiment on various building materials to determine how much downward pressure they can stand before they break.

But a building in an earthquake must withstand forces pushing it in all directions. Sometimes the ground moves upward under a building. Often the ground moves back and forth or twists the building's foundations. The builder must tie all parts of the building together carefully to withstand any possible force moving in almost any direction. And, because it is so difficult for him to experiment with these forces in a laboratory, the builder must often wait for an earthquake to strike his building before he can learn whether or not he has made a mistake.

Many scientists are trying to make instruments that will predict the coming of an earthquake. They know that the pressures that cause the rocks to slip along the fault slowly build up over a period of time. Sooner or later the pressure will become too great and the rocks will break loose suddenly and violently. So far, these studies have not been very successful. However, scientists in both Japan and the United States are working together on this problem and are making progress. Someday, perhaps within the next few years, we will be able to predict when a large earthquake will occur far enough in advance to save many lives.

Other experiments are being tried that may prevent serious earthquakes entirely by causing small, less dangerous ones. In the western part of the United States, scientists are using water to cause small rock slippages—a little at a time—along faults, thus hoping to avoid one large slip, or quake. To do this, holes are drilled into the face of the fault. Measured quantities of water are then pumped into the crack between the rocks. The water makes the fault face slippery and adds weight to the rocks on one side of the fault. The rocks are thus caused to slide a little way and to release some of the pressure that is building up. A problem facing the scientists, however, is determining how much water is needed to cause a desirable, small rock slippage.

Perhaps the most interesting aspects of the science of earthquakes are those things that we do not yet understand. People who are caught in an earthquake often report sights and sounds that scientists cannot explain. For example, you have read about several reports of waves passing through the ground or through other solid objects as the earthquake shocks pass. These waves have been described as looking much like "swells in ocean water" and, when they are in the ground, seem to be coming from the direction of the source of the earthquake. Earthquakes do send out waves through the earth, of course, but these waves are traveling at thousands of miles-per-hour and it seems unlikely that they could be seen.

Similar waves have reportedly been seen traveling along pavement and up and down smoke stacks and chimneys made of brick. One scientist was in his California laboratory during an earthquake and watched what he described as waves six

inches high ripple through the concrete floor.
After the quake, he examined the floor with a
magnifying glass and found no new cracks at all!
It has been suggested that the seeing of waves like
these is an optical illusion caused by the violent
movement of the fluid in the ears of the person
caught in the earthquake.

Many of the sounds that people hear during an
earthquake can be easily explained. Buildings that
are being shaken creak and crack. Trees sway violently and their branches snap and groan. Water
and air are pushed from loose soil by the shaking.
But other sounds are more difficult to explain.
Steady roaring sounds "coming from beneath the
earth" are often described. And a few people have
reported hearing the roaring of the earthquake
before the earth beneath them begins to shake.
Dogs, cats, and other animals sometimes seem to
be able to sense the coming of an earthquake,
sometimes several hours before the shaking is felt
by human beings.

But the most difficult question about
earthquakes that scientists must answer is, "What
causes earthquakes?" We know, of course, that
earthquakes are caused when rocks slip along
faults. But why do the rocks slip? Where does the
pressure that pushes them come from?

This mystery may be about to be solved. Geologists have recently developed a new understanding
of the crust of the earth that leads them to believe
that perhaps earthquakes, volcanoes, and mountains are all caused by the same forces within the

earth. As you have seen as you read this book, most earthquakes occur in the same regions of the earth in which volcanoes are usually found. And these regions are located near mountains that have only recently in the history of the earth been pushed up from the sea.

Putting together a great deal of evidence from many sources, geologists have developed a new theory about how our earth got the face that it has. According to this theory, the earth's surface is divided into segments called *plates.*

No one can be certain at this time how many plates the earth's surface is divided into. Although some scientists think that there may be as many as 20 or more, most experts agree that there are at least six to eight major plates. One plate contains all of Europe and Asia. Another underlies almost all of the Pacific Ocean. A third plate contains Africa. A fourth is under the Indian Ocean and includes the land areas of Australia and India. A fifth major plate includes Antarctica and much of the nearby ocean. North America and the Arctic region are on the same plate, which extends eastward to the center of the Atlantic Ocean. Some geologists feel that the South American Continent is on the same plate, while others draw their maps in such a way as to show South America and the western part of the South Atlantic Ocean to be on a separate, seventh plate.

How many plates there actually are is not very important to us right now. The important thing is that at least some of them are actually moving.

Like huge rafts, thousands of miles across and
between 20 and 100 miles deep, the plates seem
to be floating on the almost-liquid rocks below.
The movement is, as you might expect, very
slow—perhaps only an inch or so a year at the
most. But when we look at a map of the plates
and a map of the major earthquake belts of the
earth, there is a remarkable similarity. The
earthquake belts of the earth occur at or close to
the edges of the major plates—where they meet.
In the North Atlantic, for example, most
earthquakes occur along the Mid-Atlantic Ridge,
the boundary of the North American Plate and
the Eurasian Plate. Not only do earthquakes occur
along the Mid-Atlantic Ridge, but volcanoes also
are common on the Ridge. In fact most of the
earth's volcanoes and major mountain ranges
seem to occur along the edges of these plates. So,
perhaps, even the very slow movement of some of
the major plates of the earth's surface can help us
to explain earthquakes, volcanoes, and even
mountain building.

For example, let us consider the plate upon
which North America rides. This huge piece of
the earth's crust extends from the Mid-Atlantic
Ridge to the western edge of the continent. On
its western edge, along the west coast of the
United States and Canada, this plate touches the
huge plate upon which the Pacific Ocean rests.
The North American Plate is being pushed steadily toward the west. The Pacific Plate, on the other
hand, seems to be moving in a north-westerly

direction. What must happen where these two plates meet?

Some geologists think that the North American Plate is overriding the edge of the Pacific Plate. As the two plates grind against each other, these scientists suggest, the edge of the Pacific Plate is forced deeper and deeper beneath North America. At the same time, the western edge of the North American Plate is pushed slightly upward. As this happens, the rocks of the upper plate fold and fault.

One result of this type of movement would be the formation of mountains. We might picture the mountains that line the western edge of the American continents as being wrinkles in the crust of the earth caused by the pressure of one plate's edge against that of its neighbor.

Another result of this kind of movement would certainly be earthquakes. The edge of the North American Plate does not follow the coastline exactly, but swings inland somewhere between Los Angeles and San Francisco. Apparently, then, Los Angeles rides on the edge of the Pacific Plate and is moving slowly toward the northwest. San Francisco, on the other hand, sits on the edge of the North American Plate and is being pushed almost due west. The edges of these two plates are marked by the mountains of the coast and by the hundreds of faults that crisscross the area. As the plates push against each other pressure builds higher and higher. Sooner or later this pressure becomes too great and the plates suddenly slip a little. The result is an earthquake.

If we accept the theory of plates we can answer the question of where the pressure comes from that causes earthquakes. But now we are faced with an even more difficult question. Where does the pressure come from that moves the *plates*? It would require a tremendous amount of energy to move even the smallest of the earth's plates even a fraction of an inch. What a gigantic force it must take to move an entire continent and half an ocean!

Geologists think they may have an answer to this question, too. It is a well-accepted idea that the interior of the earth is very, very hot. Actually, it seems likely that the temperatures of the rocks deep within the earth are higher than the melting point of the rocks. But the rocks are probably not liquid because of the tremendous pressure from the weight of the rocks above them. Therefore, scientists assume that these deep rocks do not flow like a liquid does. But they probably would change shape slowly if uneven pressure were put on them.

So we can picture the material upon which the plates rest as being made up of almost-liquid rock that is very hot. Now suppose that one section of this rock becomes heated more than the other sections around it. This overheated rock would expand and take up more space. Each cubic foot of the expanded rock would weigh less than it did before, since it now contains less material. The less dense rock would then slowly—very, very slowly—start to rise toward the surface.

As it neared the surface, the pressure on the rock would become less and less and it would become more liquid. If the liquid came in contact with a fault, a volcano would be produced and lava would be forced out onto the surface. This, scientists suggest, would be the edge of a plate. The liquid rock would then spread out along both sides of the fault, cooling and becoming more dense as it moved away from the source of heat. As time passed, this material would be carried away from the fault as the plate moved. Being heavier now, it would eventually sink back into the earth, probably in one of the many *trenches* that cut the ocean floors around the earth.

It is this movement of material from inside the earth that is thought to carry the continents along. For example, it is suggested that the Mid-Atlantic Ridge is being formed by lava rising to the surface along a huge series of faults, and that the North American Plate is being carried westward by the current in the rocks. The plates that contain Europe and Africa are being carried toward the east by the material flowing from the Ridge.

These ideas are *hypotheses*, educated guesses based on much accumulated data. And we can be certain that many more interesting ideas will be suggested before the geologists agree that they understand the causes of earthquakes. Meanwhile, more studies of earthquakes are being made. And as a result of these studies, perhaps a better understanding of the causes and effects of earthquakes will come about. Then, someday, man may perhaps be able to predict, live with, and even control this tremendous force of nature.

INDEX

About the Authors

Billye Walker Brown maintains a furious schedule of activity to keep up with all her interests. When she's not researching and writing about historical catastrophes, she edits other peoples' book manuscripts. Mrs. Brown keeps in touch with young people through her three teenage daughters and their friends.

Walter Brown has his Ph.D. in science education from The Ohio State University and enjoys teaching junior high school students. He has co-authored a science textbook series that is used in many junior high school science courses throughout the country.